Contents

Name _____

A B C D E F G H I J K L M N O P Q R S T U V W X Y Z
a b c d e f g h i j k l m n o p q r s t u v w x y z

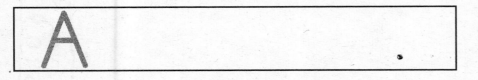 A

 a

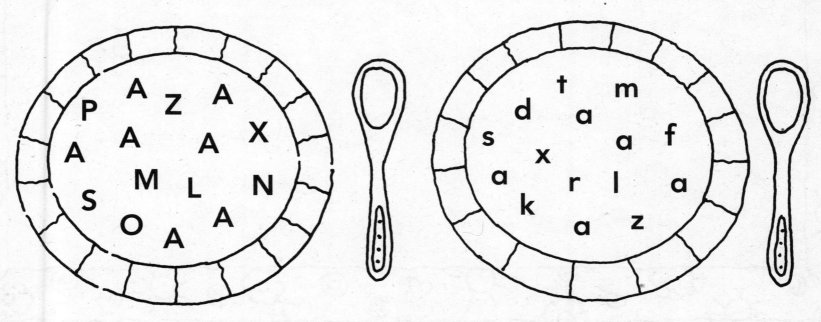

Children

- write *A* and *a* in the boxes
- circle all the *A*'s in the left bowl of alphabet soup
- circle all the *a*'s in the right bowl of alphabet soup

HOME CONNECTION

I am learning about big and small *Aa*. Let me show you all the big *A*'s and small *a*'s in the alphabet soup.

1

Name _____

Children

• write their names
• draw pictures of themselves

 HOME CONNECTION

I am learning to write my name.
Help me write it at home, too.

2

Name _____

A B C D E F G H I J K L M N O P Q R S T U V W X Y Z
a b c d e f g h i j k l m n o p q r s t u v w x y z

B

b

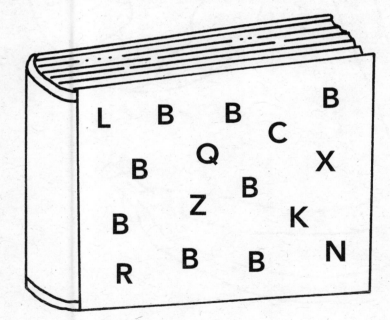

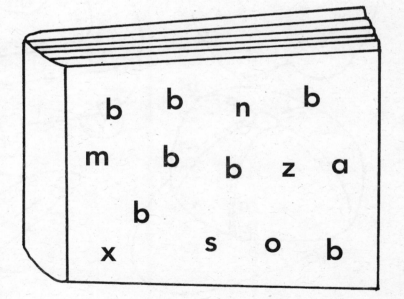

Children

- write *B* and *b* in the boxes
- circle all the *B*'s in the first book
- circle all the *b*'s in the second book

 HOME CONNECTION

I am learning about big and small *Bb*.
Let me show you all the big *B*'s and
small *b*'s in the books.

3

 Welcome to **Kindergarten**

Name _____

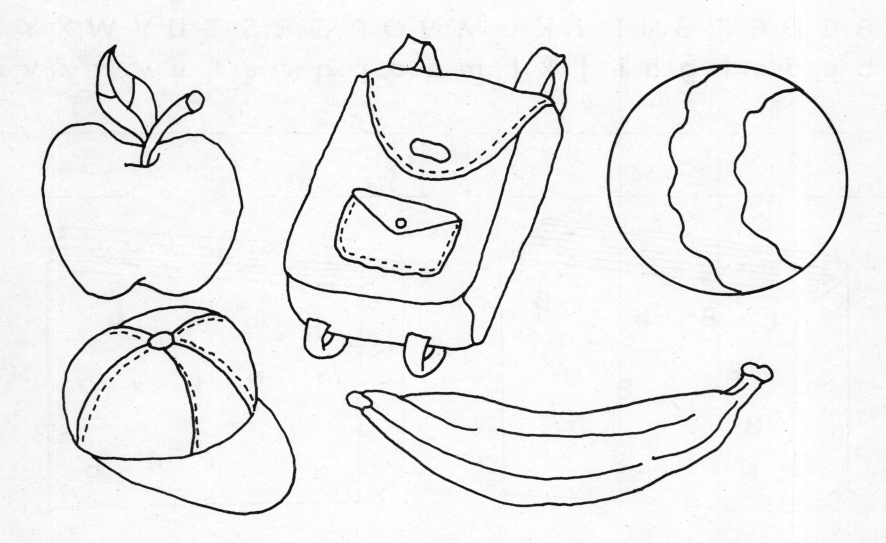

Children

- color the apple red, the banana yellow, the cap blue, the ball green, and the backpack orange
- say the names of the colors

 HOME CONNECTION

I am learning colors. Ask me to name the colors I know so far. Help me learn some new ones!

4

Welcome to
Kindergarten

Name _____

A B C D E F G H I J K L M N O P Q R S T U V W X Y Z

a b c d e f g h i j k l m n o p q r s t u v w x y z

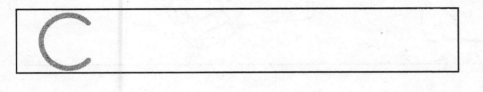

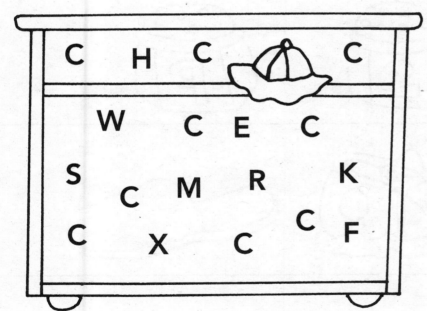

Children

- write *C* and *c* in the boxes
- circle all the *C*'s in the first cubby
- circle all the *c*'s in the next cubby

 HOME CONNECTION

I am learning about big and small *Cc*.
Let me show you all the big *C*'s and
small *c*'s in the cubbies.

5

Name _____

1.

2.

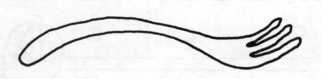  

3.

 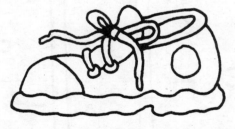 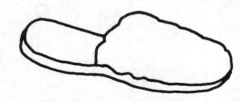

Children

- circle two things that go together in each row
- name the pair

 HOME CONNECTION

I am learning about things that go together. Help me find pairs of things at home.

6

Welcome to Kindergarten

Name _____

A B C D E F G H I J K L M N O P Q R S T U V W X Y Z
a b c d e f g h i j k l m n o p q r s t u v w x y z

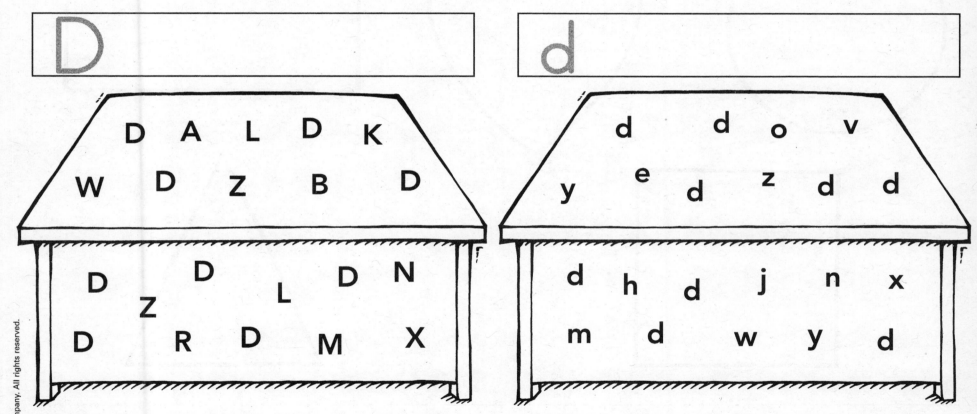

D

d

Children

- write _D_ and _d_ in the boxes
- circle all the _D_'s on the first desk
- circle all the _d_'s on the next desk

HOME CONNECTION

I am learning about big and small _Dd_.
Let me show you all the big _D_'s
and small _d_'s on the desks.

7

Welcome to Kindergarten

Name _____

Children

- find the circle and color it red
- find the triangle and color it blue
- find the rectangle and color it yellow
- find the square and color it brown

 HOME CONNECTION

I am learning about shapes. Help me find these shapes in things at home.

8

Welcome to
Kindergarten

Name _____

A B C D E F G H I J K L M N O P Q R S T U V W X Y Z

a b c d e f g h i j k l m n o p q r s t u v w x y z

E

e

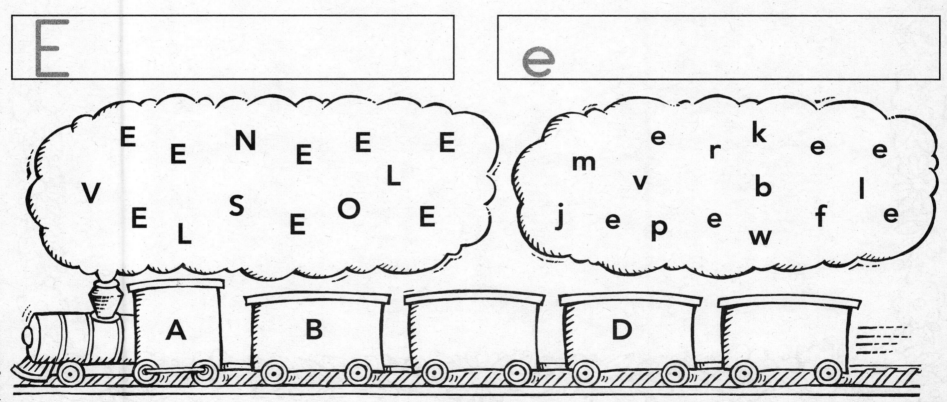

Children

- write _E_ and _e_ in the boxes
- circle all the _E_'s and _e_'s in the steam from the engine
- write the missing capital letters on the alphabet train

HOME CONNECTION

I am learning about big and small _Ee_. Let me show you all the big _E_'s and small _e_'s in the picture. Then let's read the letters on the alphabet train.

9

Welcome to
Kindergarten

Name _____

Children

- write all the letters they know
- point to each letter and name it

HOME CONNECTION

I can write some letters. Sing the "Alphabet Song" with me. Then help me write all the letters in my name.

Welcome to
Kindergarten

Name _____

A B C D E F G H I J K L M N O P Q R S T U V W X Y Z
a b c d e f g h i j k l m n o p q r s t u v w x y z

F

f

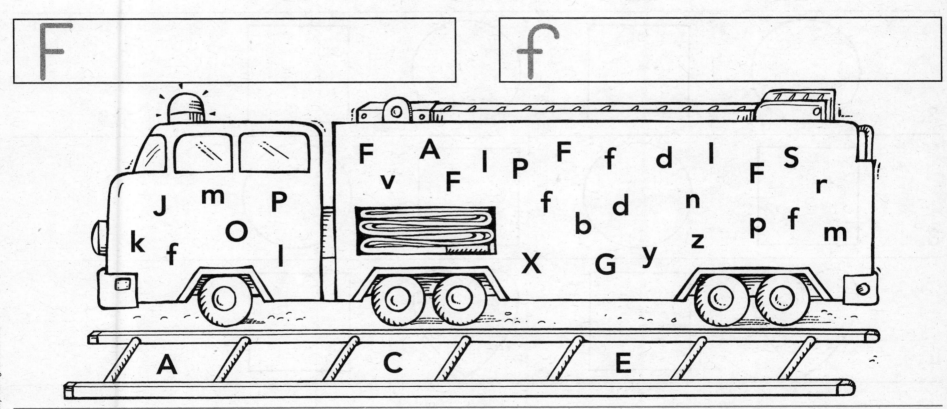

Children

- write *F* and *f* in the boxes
- circle all the *F*'s and *f*'s on the fire engine
- write the missing capital letters on the alphabet ladder

 HOME CONNECTION

I am learning about big and small *Ff*. Let me show you all the big *F*'s and small *f*'s on the fire engine. Then let's read the letters on the alphabet ladder.

11

Welcome to
Kindergarten

Name _____

1.

2.

3.

4.

Children
- name the pictures in each row
- draw what comes next in the pattern

 HOME CONNECTION

I am learning about patterns. Can we find some patterns at home? (Hint: Clothing or wallpaper with stripes is a good place to start!)

Name _____

A B C D E F G H I J K L M N O P Q R S T U V W X Y Z
a b c d e f g h i j k l m n o p q r s t u v w x y z

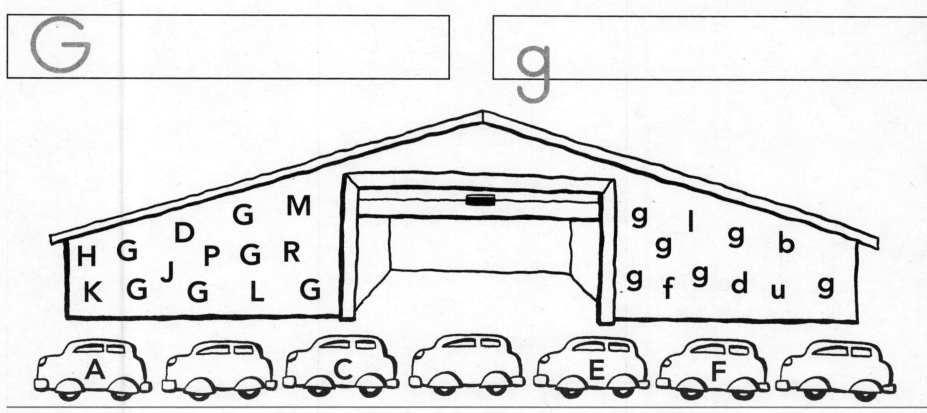

Children

• write *G* and *g* in the boxes
• circle all the *G*'s and *g*'s on the garage
• write the missing capital letters on the alphabet cars

 HOME CONNECTION

I am learning about big and small *Gg*.
Let me show you all the big *G*'s and
small *g*'s on the garage. Then let's read
the letters on the alphabet cars.

Name _____

1	2	3

Children

- say each number
- draw balloons to show the number

HOME CONNECTION

I am learning to count. Help me count things as I set the table.

14

Welcome to Kindergarten

Name _____

A B C D E F G H I J K L M N O P Q R S T U V W X Y Z

a b c d e f g h i j k l m n o p q r s t u v w x y z

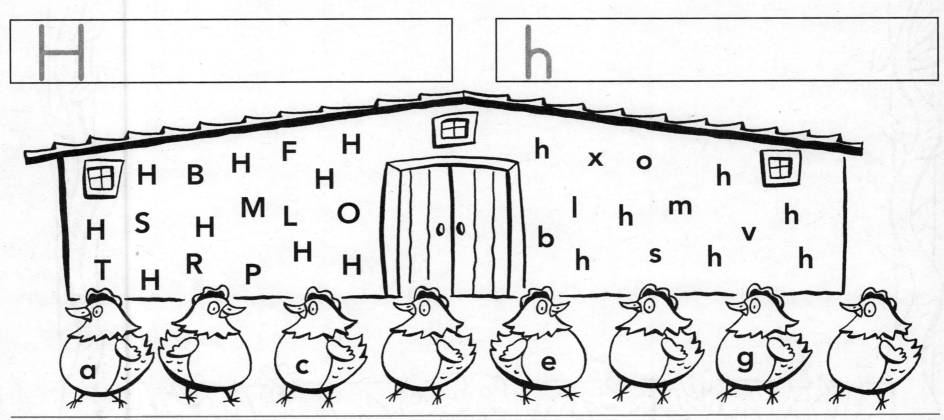

Children

- write *H* and *h* in the boxes
- circle all the *H*'s and *h*'s on the henhouse
- write the missing small letters on the alphabet hens

HOME CONNECTION

I am learning about big and small *Hh*.
Let me show you all the big *H*'s and
small *h*'s on the henhouse. Then let's
read the letters on the alphabet hens.

15

Welcome to Kindergarten

Name _____

Children

- write the numbers 1 to 10
- write more numbers if they can

 HOME CONNECTION

I am learning to write numbers.
Help me write them at home, too.

Name _____

A B C D E F G H I J K L M N O P Q R S T U V W X Y Z

a b c d e f g h i j k l m n o p q r s t u v w x y z

I		i

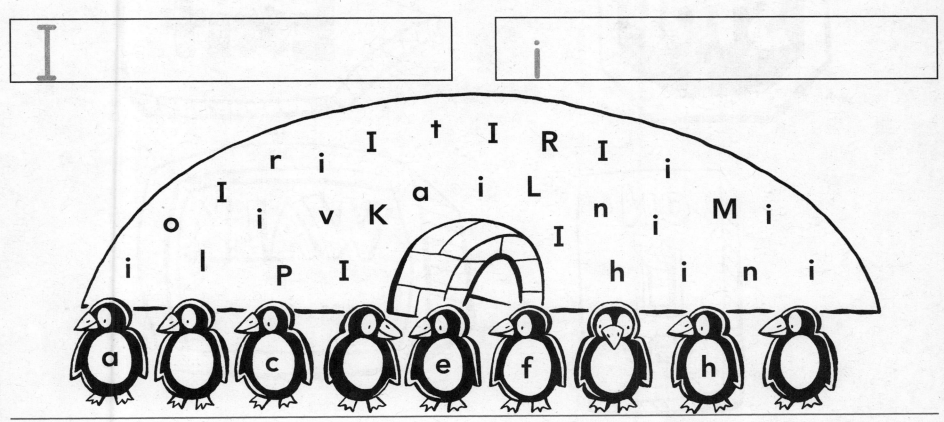

Children

- write *I* and *i* in the boxes
- circle all the *I*'s and *i*'s on the igloo
- write the missing lowercase letters on the alphabet penguins

 HOME CONNECTION

I am learning about big and small *Ii*. Let me show you all the big *I*'s and small *i*'s on the igloo. Then let's read the letters on the alphabet penguins.

17

Welcome to Kindergarten

Name _____

Children

- tell what they see in each picture
- say what the sign tells them to do

HOME CONNECTION

I am learning about signs. Let's look for these signs when we go out together.

Welcome to
Kindergarten

Name _____

A B C D E F G H I J K L M N O P Q R S T U V W X Y Z

a b c d e f g h i j k l m n o p q r s t u v w x y z

J

j

Children

- write *J* and *j* in the boxes
- circle all the *J*'s and *j*'s on the jet
- write the missing lowercase letters on the alphabet carts

 HOME CONNECTION

I am learning about big and small *Jj*. Let me show you all the big *J*'s and small *j*'s on the jet. Then let's read the letters on the alphabet carts.

19

Welcome to
Kindergarten

Name _____

 Children

• write all the words they know how to write
• read each word they've written

 HOME CONNECTION

I can write some words. Let me read them to you.

Name _____

THEME 1: Look at Us!
Week One *Now I'm Big*
Compare and Contrast, Responding

Children
- look at the pictures of things babies eat, wear, ride, and play with
- draw pictures of things they eat, wear, ride, and play with

 Home Connection
Let me tell you about a book called *Now I'm Big*. Then I can tell you how my pictures show I've grown.

21

Name _____

ABCDEFGHIJKLMNOPQRSTUVWXYZ
abcdefghijklmnopqrstuvwxyz

K

k

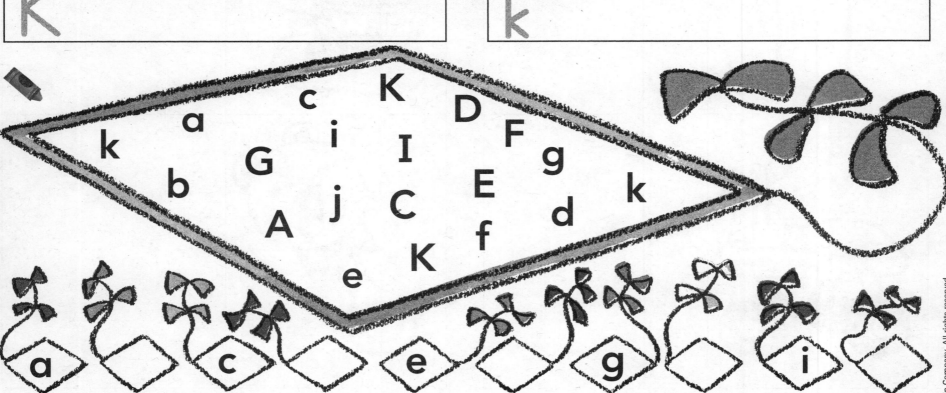

THEME 1: Look at Us!
Week One
Letter Name Kk

Children
• write K and k in the boxes
• circle all the K's and k's on the kite
• write the missing lowercase letters on the small kites

Home Connection
I am learning about big and small Kk. Let me show you all the big K's and small k's on the kite. Then let's read the letters on the alphabet kites.

22

Name _____

ABCDEFGHIJKLMNOPQRSTUVWXYZ

abcdefghijklmnopqrstuvwxyz

L

l

a   l   C   B   G   F

c   d   l   i   h   L

H   L   b   D   E   l

K   G   J   g   e   A

j   k   f

a   b   d   f   h   j   k

THEME 1: Look at Us!
Week One
Letter Name *Ll*

Children
- write *L* and *l* in the boxes
- circle all the *L*'s and *l*'s on the lion
- write the missing lowercase letters on the small lions

 Home Connection
I am learning about big and small *Ll*. Let me show you all the big *L*'s and small *l*'s on the lion. Then let's read the letters on the small lions.

23

Name _____

THEME 1: Look at Us!
Week One *Mice Squeak, We Speak*
Compare and Contrast, Responding

Children
- circle an animal that squeaks
- color green an animal that croaks
- circle an animal that moos
- color yellow an animal that quacks
- underline those who can speak

 Home Connection
Let me tell you a story called *Mice Squeak, We Speak*. Then I can tell you what my picture shows.

24

Name _____

ABCDEFGHIJKLMNOPQRSTUVWXYZ

abcdefghijklmnopqrstuvwxyz

M

m

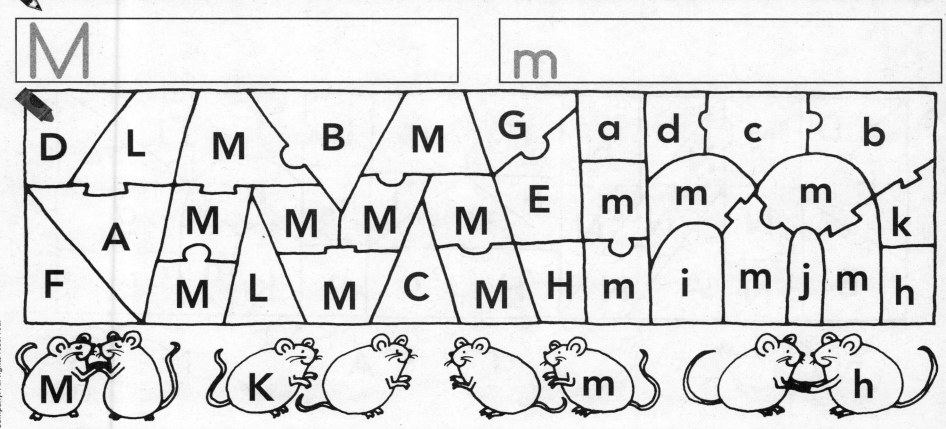

THEME 1: Look at Us!
Week One
Letter Name _Mm_

Children
- color every puzzle piece with _M_ red
- color every puzzle piece with _m_ blue
- see what shapes the red and blue pieces make
- write the matching capital or lowercase letter on the mice

 Home Connection
I am learning about big and small _Mm_. Let me show you all the big _M_'s and small _m_'s on the puzzle. Then let's read the matching letters on the mice.

25

ABCDEFGHIJKLMNOPQRSTUVWXYZ

abcdefghijklmnopqrstuvwxyz

N

n

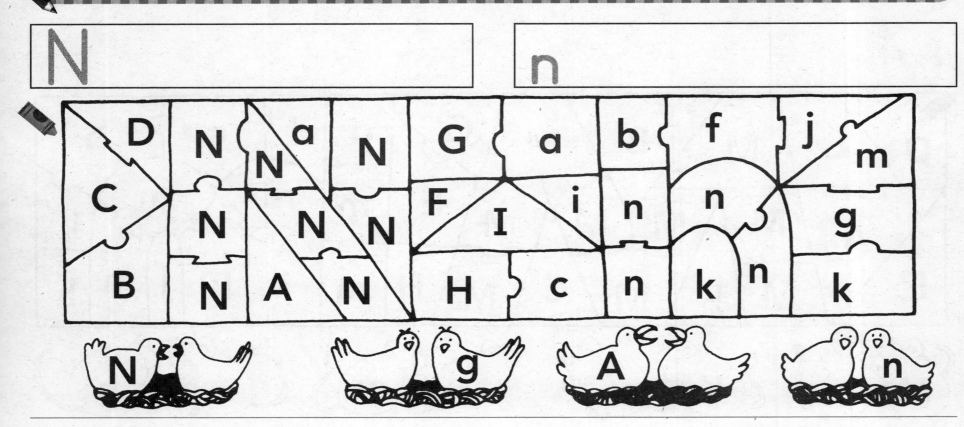

THEME 1: Look at Us!
Week One
Letter Name Nn

Children
- color every puzzle piece with *N* green
- color every puzzle piece with *n* yellow
- see what shapes the green and yellow pieces make
- write the matching capital or lowercase letter on the birds

 Home Connection
I am learning about big and small *Nn*. Let me show you all the big *N*'s and small *n*'s on the puzzle. Then let's read the matching letters on the birds.

Name _____

A B C D E F G H I J K L M N O P Q R S T U V W X Y Z
a b c d e f g h i j k l m n o p q r s t u v w x y z

THEME 1: Look at Us!
Week One
Letter Name *Oo*

Children
- color every puzzle piece with *O* purple
- color every puzzle piece with *o* orange
- see what shapes the purple and orange pieces make
- write the matching capital or lowercase letter on the octopuses

Home Connection
I am learning about big and small *Oo*. Let me show you all the big *O*'s and small *o*'s on the puzzle. Then let's read the matching letters on the octopuses.

27

28   Just for fun, color the gingerbread people! What colors did you choose?

Name _____

1.

2.

THEME 1: Look At Us!
Week Two *The Gingerbread Man*
Noting Important Details

Children
- color the cookie that looks like the Gingerbread Man in the story
- color the characters who chased after the Gingerbread Man

 Home Connection
Let me tell you the story *The Gingerbread Man*.

Name _____

THEME 1: Look at Us!
Week Two *The Gingerbread Man*
Responding

Children
• decorate their own gingerbread man

 Home Connection
Today I decorated this gingerbread man. Maybe some weekend we could make gingerbread cookies together!

Name _____

ABCDEFGHIJKLMNOPQRSTUVWXYZ

abcdefghijklmnopqrstuvwxyz

P	p

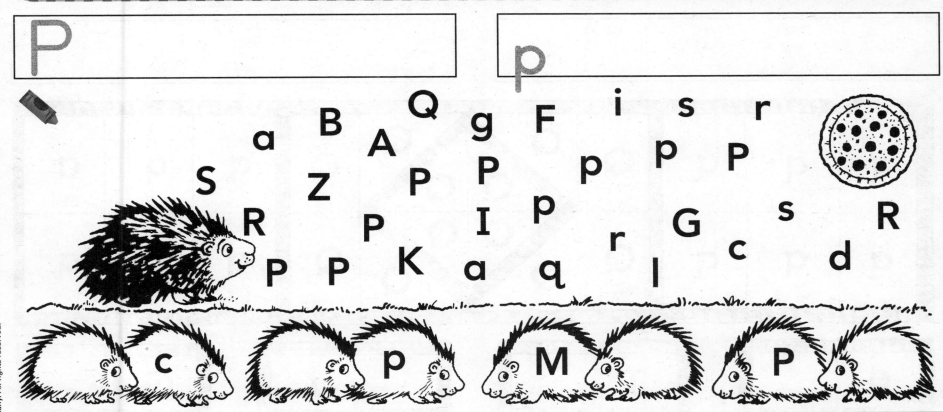

THEME 1: Look at Us!
Week Two
Letter Name _Pp_

Children

- write _P_ and _p_ in the boxes
- circle all the _P_'s and _p_'s on the path
- color the circles to show Porcupine the path to the pizza
- write the matching capital or lowercase letter on the small porcupines

Home Connection

I am learning about big and small _Pp_. Let me show you all the big _P_'s and small _p_'s on the path. Then let's read the matching letters on the small porcupines.

31

Name _____

ABCDEFGHIJKLMNOPQRSTUVWXYZ

abcdefghijklmnopqrstuvwxyz

Q

q

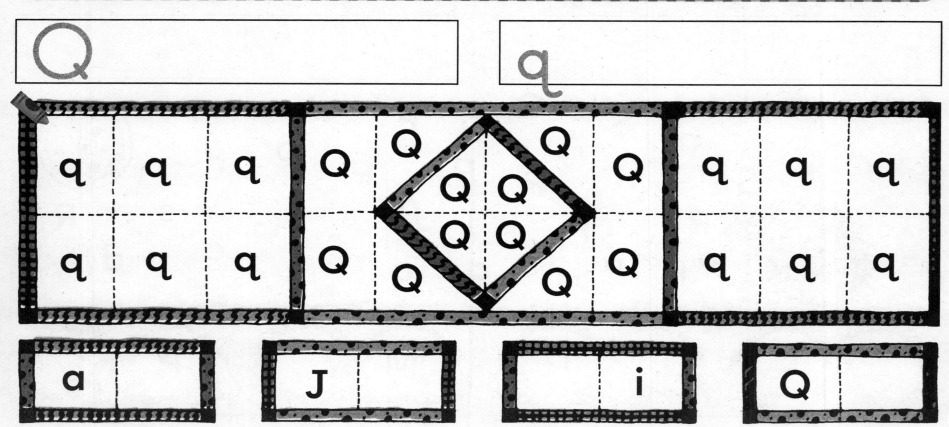

| q | q | q | Q | Q | Q | Q | Q | Q | q | q | q |
| q | q | q | Q | Q | Q | Q | Q | Q | q | q | q |

| a | | | J | | | | i | | Q | |

THEME 1: Look at Us!
Week Two
Letter Name *Qq*

Children
- write *Q* and *q* in the boxes
- color all the *Q*'s red
- color all the *q*'s blue
- write the matching capital or lowercase letter on the quilt squares

 Home Connection
I am learning about big and small *Qq*. Let me show you all the big *Q*'s and small *q*'s on the quilt. Then let's read the matching letters on the quilt squares.

32

Name _____

THEME 1: Look at Us!
Week Two _Here Are My Hands_
Noting Important Details

Children
• circle the body parts named in the book
• draw a picture of themselves, adding as much detail as they can

Home Connection
Let me tell you about the book _Here Are My Hands_. Then I can tell you about this picture I drew of myself.

Name _____

R

r

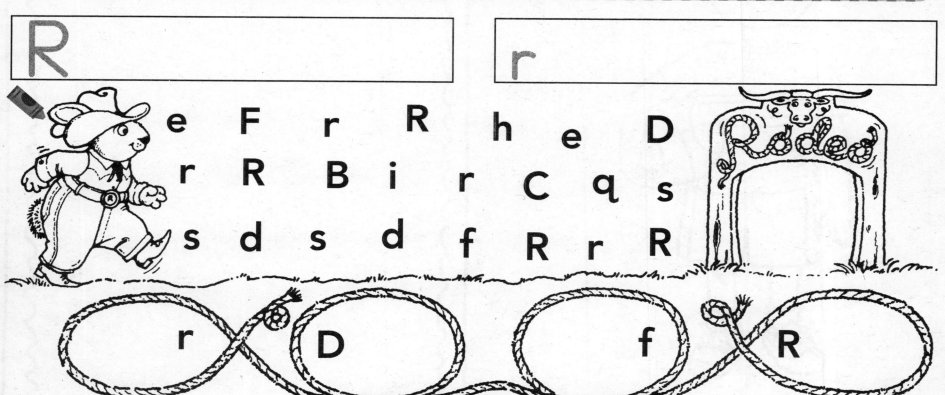

e F r R h e D

r R B i r C q s

s d s d f R r R

r D f R

THEME 1: Look at Us!
Week Two
Letter Name *Rr*

Children
- write *R* and *r* in the boxes
- circle all the *R*'s and *r*'s on the path
- color the circles to show Rabbit the path to the rodeo
- write the matching capital or lowercase letter in the ropes

 Home Connection
I am learning about big and small *Rr*. Let me show you all the big *R*'s and small *r*'s on the path. Then let's read the matching letters in the ropes.

34

Name _____

ABCDEFGHIJKLMNOPQRSTUVWXYZ
abcdefghijklmnopqrstuvwxyz

| S | | s |

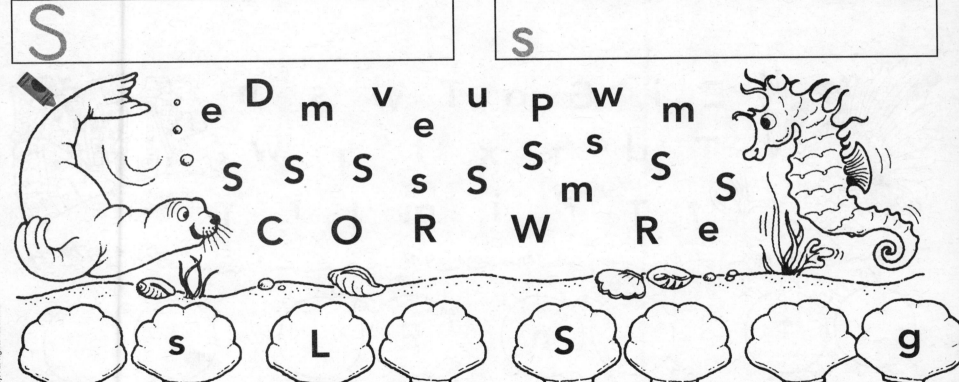

| S | L | | S | | g |

THEME 1: Look at Us!
Week Two
Letter Name *Ss*

Children
- write *S* and *s* in the boxes
- circle all the *S*'s and *s*'s on the path
- color the circles to show Seal the path to the seahorse
- write the matching capital or lowercase letter on the shells

Home Connection
I am learning about big and small *Ss*. Let me show you all the big *S*'s and small *s*'s on the path. Then let's read the matching letters on the shells.

35

Name _____

ABCDEFGHIJKLMNOPQRSTUVWXYZ
abcdefghijklmnopqrstuvwxyz

T | | t

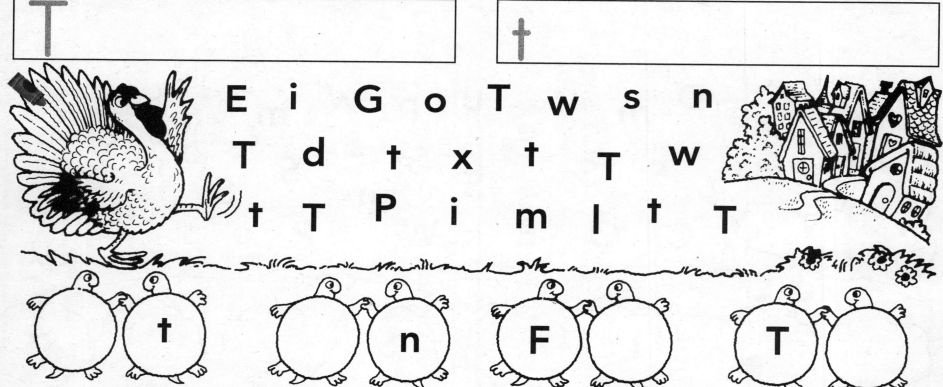

E i G o T w s n

T d t x t T W

t T P i m l t T

t | n | F | T

THEME 1: Look at Us!
Week Two
Letter Name *Tt*

Children
• write *T* and *t* in the boxes
• circle all the *T*'s and *t*'s on the path
• color the circles to show Turkey the path to the town
• write the matching capital or lowercase letter on the turtles

Home Connection
I am learning about big and small *Tt*. Let me show you all the big *T*'s and small *t*'s on the path. Then let's read the matching letters on the turtles.

Name _____

Theme 1: Look at Us!
Week Three *The City Mouse and the Country Mouse*
Compare and Contrast

Children
- think about the differences between the city and country scenes
- color the scene that is more like where they live

 Home Connection
Let me tell you about *The City Mouse and the Country Mouse* and why I colored this picture.

37

ABCDEFGHIJKLMNOPQRSTUVWXYZ
abcdefghijklmnopqrstuvwxyz

U

u

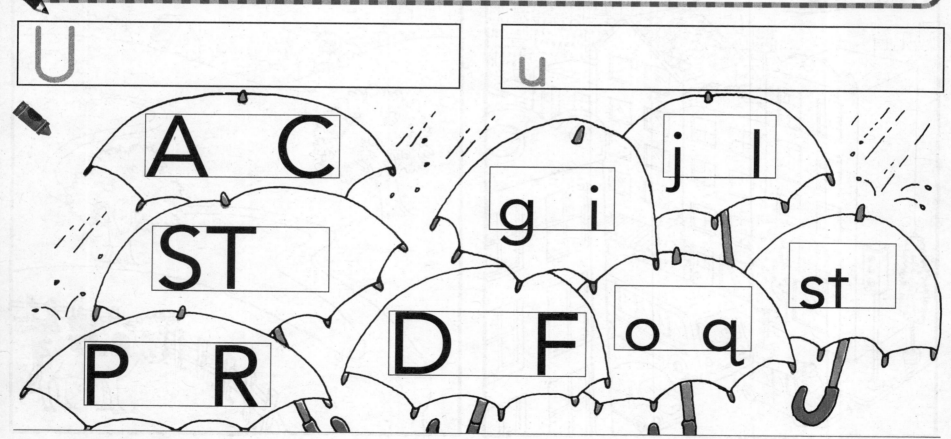

THEME 1: Look at Us!
Week Three
Letter Name *Uu*

Children
• write *U* and *u* in the boxes
• write the missing letters on the umbrellas

 Home Connection
I am learning about big and small *Uu*. Let me show you all the big *U*'s and small *u*'s on the umbrellas. Then let's read the sets of three letters on the umbrellas.

Name _____

ABCDEFGHIJKLMNOPQRSTUVWXYZ
abcdefghijklmnopqrstuvwxyz

V

v

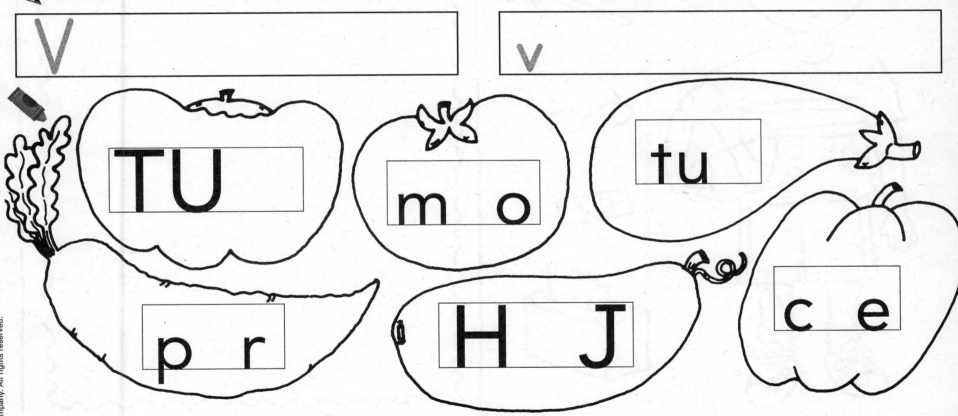

TU

m   o

tu

p r

H J

c e

THEME 1: Look at Us!
Week Three
Letter Name Vv

Children
• write *V* and *v* in the boxes
• write the missing letters on the vegetables

Home Connection
I am learning about big and small *Vv*. Let me show you all the big *V*'s and small *v*'s on the vegetables. Then let's read the sets of three letters on the vegetables.

39

Name _____

1.

2.

Copyright © Houghton Mifflin Company. All rights reserved.

THEME 1: Look at Us!
Week Three *Here Are My Hands*
Noting Important Details

40

Children

1. draw lines from a body part to the object that goes with it

2. draw a picture of something they do with their hands, adding as much detail as they can

 Home Connection
Let me tell you about the picture I drew. Let's think of other things I can do with my hands.

Name _____

ABCDEFGHIJKLMNOPQRSTUVWXYZ
abcdefghijklmnopqrstuvwxyz

W

w

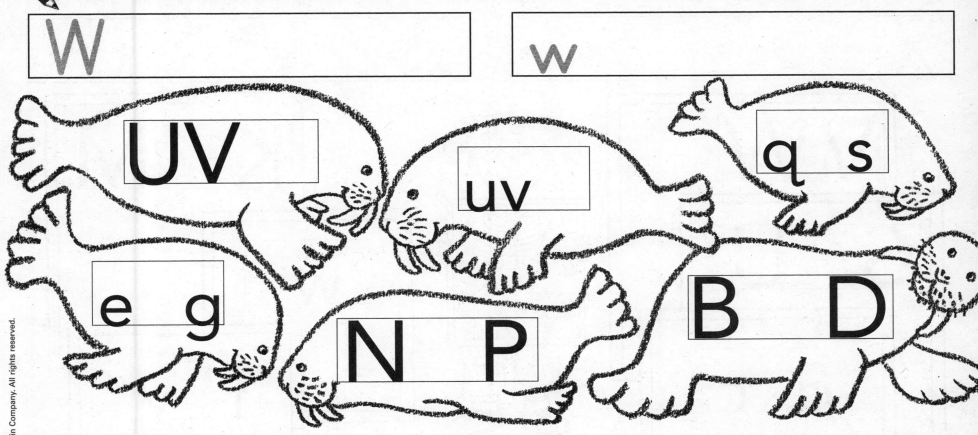

UV

uv

q   s

e   g

N   P

B   D

THEME 1: Look at Us!
Week Three
Letter Name *Ww*

Children
• write *W* and *w* in the boxes
• write the missing letters on the walruses

 Home Connection
I am learning about big and
small *Ww*. Let me show you all
the big *W*'s and small *w*'s on the
walruses. Then let's read the sets
of three letters on the walruses.

41

Name _____

ABCDEFGHIJKLMNOPQRSTUVWXYZ
abcdefghijklmnopqrstuvwxyz

X

x

THEME 1: Look at Us!
Week Three
Letter Name Xx

Children
- write *X* and *x* in the boxes
- write the missing letters on the x-rays

 Home Connection
I am learning about big and small *Xx*. Let me show you all the big *X*'s and small *x*'s on the x-rays. Then let's read the sets of three letters on the x-rays.

Name _____

A B C D E F G H I J K L M N O P Q R S T U V W X Y Z

a b c d e f g h i j k l m n o p q r s t u v w x y z

Y

y

W X

wx

k m

T V

p r

G I

THEME 1: Look at Us!
Week Three
Letter Name *Yy*

Children
• write *Y* and *y* in the boxes
• write the missing letters on the yaks

 Home Connection
I am learning about big and
small *Yy*. Let me show you all
the big *Y*'s and small *y*'s on the
yaks. Then let's read the sets of
three letters on the yaks.

43

Name _____

ABCDEFGHIJKLMNOPQRSTUVWXYZ

abcdefghijklmnopqrstuvwxyz

Z

z

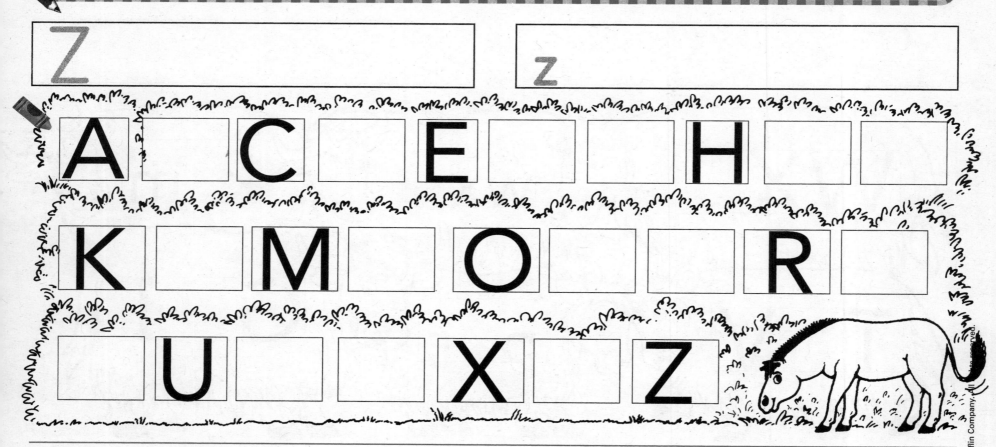

A   C   E   H

K   M   O   R

U   X   Z

THEME 1: Look at Us!
Week Three
Letter Name *Zz*

Children
- write Z and z in the boxes
- write the missing letters on the alphabet bushes
- color the stripes on the zebra

 Home Connection
I am learning about big and small *Zz*. Let's read the whole alphabet that ends with the zebra. Then I'll show you the big Z and the zebra I colored.

44

Name _____

1   2   3

THEME 2: Colors All Around
Week One *I Need a Lunch Box*
Sequence of Events

Children
- think about what happened in the story
- write 1, 2, or 3 beside the pictures to show what happened first, next, and last
- color the pictures

 Home Connection
Let me tell you what happened in the story *I Need a Lunch Box*. We can point to the pictures as I tell each part.

45

Name _____

Monday

Tuesday

Wednesday

Thursday

Friday

THEME 2: Colors All Around
Week One *I Need a Lunch Box*
Responding

Children
- draw a different lunch box for each school day
- color each one a different color

Home Connection
Help me say the names of the days I go to school. Then I'll tell you about the lunch boxes I drew and the colors I used.

46

Name _____

THEME 2: Colors All Around
Week One
Phonemic Awareness: /s/

Children
- color all the pictures on pages 47 and 48 whose names start like *Sammy Seal*
- cut and paste pictures for that sound in the boxes on page 48

 Home Connection
Let's name all the things on the front and back whose names start like *Sammy Seal*.

47

Name _____

THEME 2: Colors All Around
Week One
Phonemic Awareness: /s/

Name _____

1.  **S** **S**s **S** _ _ _ _ _ _ **s** _ _ _ _ _ _   _ _ _ _ _ _   _ _ _ _ _ _

2.

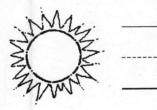 _ _ _ _ _ _ _ _ _   _ _ _ _ _ _ _ _ _

 _ _ _ _ _ _ _ _ _    _ _ _ _ _ _ _ _ _

 _ _ _ _ _ _ _ _ _    _ _ _ _ _ _ _ _ _

3.

THEME 2: Colors All Around
Week One
Phonics: Initial Consonant _s_

Children
for 1 and 2,
• write _s_ beside the pictures whose names start like _Sammy Seal_

for 3,
• draw two things whose names start with the sound for _s_

 Home Connection
Let's look at the grocery store for things whose names begin with the sound for _s._

49

Name _____

✏ 1.

I _____

.

2. _____
_____

.

3. _____
_____

.

🖍 4.

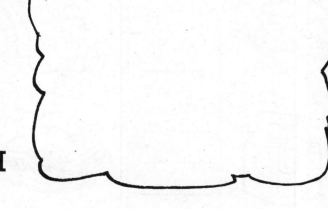

I
.

THEME 2: Colors All Around
Week One
High-Frequency Word *I*

Children
for 1, 2, and 3,
• write the word *I* to complete the sentence
for 4,
• draw a picture to complete the sentence

 Home Connection
I am learning to read the word *I*.
Let me read the sentences to
you.

50

Name _____

1.	2.	3.

THEME 2: Colors All Around
Week One *I Went Walking*
Sequence of Events, Responding

Children
- make up a story about a walk in the woods
- think about what animals of different colors they might see
- draw one animal in each of the numbered boxes
- tell a friend which animal they saw first, next, and last

 Home Connection
Let me tell you a story I made up about a walk in the woods and the animals I saw.

Name _____

S s S ___ s ___

THEME 2: Colors All Around
Week One
Phonics: Initial Consonant s

Children
• write *Ss* at the top
• name the pictures Sammy Seal thinks about
• color and write *s* beside pictures whose names begin with the sound for *s*

Home Connection
The next time we watch TV together, let's watch for things that start with the sound for *s*.

Name _____

 1.

I _____ 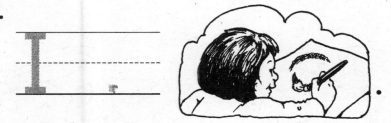 •

2. _____

_____  •

3. _____

_____  •

I

 4.

I •

THEME 2: Colors All Around
Week One
High-Frequency Word Review *I*

Children
for 1, 2, and 3,
• write the word *I* to complete the sentence
for 4,
• draw a picture to complete the sentence

 Home Connection
I am learning to read the word *I*.
Let me read the sentences to
you.

53

Just for fun, color the lunch boxes that show pictures of animals.

Name _____

THEME 2: Colors All Around
Week Two *Caps of Many Colors*
Making Predictions

Children
- think about what the monkeys did in the story
- see the monkeys watching the children
- predict what the monkeys might do with a T-shirt, a camera, and a swing
- draw pictures of their predictions

 Home Connection
Let me tell you a story called *Caps of Many Colors*. Then I'll tell you what the monkeys I drew are doing.

55

Name _____

THEME 2: Colors All Around
Week Two *Caps of Many Colors*
Responding

Children
• think about how the man in the story sold his caps
• make believe they have a shop that sells hats
• draw and color hats they might sell

 Home Connection
Let me tell you about the hats I might sell if I had a hat shop. Which hat is your favorite? Maybe we can draw more hats together.

Name _____

THEME 2: Colors All Around
Week Two
Phonemic Awareness: /m/

Children
- fix and color all the pictures on pages 57 and 58 whose names start like *Mimi Mouse*
- cut and paste pictures for that sound in the boxes on page 58
- draw something else whose name starts with that sound

 Home Connection
Let's name all the things on the front and back whose names start like *Mimi Mouse*.

Name _____

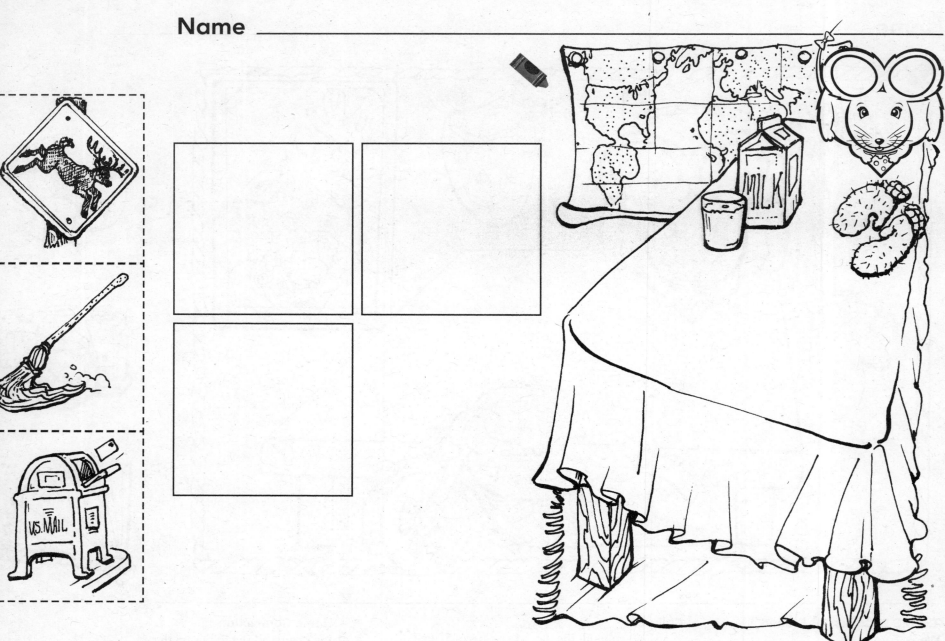

Name _____

THEME 2: Colors All Around
Week Two
Phonics: Initial Consonant *m*

Children
- draw lines from pictures whose names start with the sound for *m* to *Mm*
- write *Mm* and draw something else for that sound in the box with Mimi Mouse

 Home Connection
Let me tell you which picture names start with the sound for *m*. Then let's look in a magazine for things whose names start with the sound for *m*.

59

Name _____

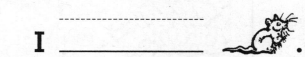

I see

1. **I see**  .

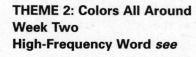

2. _____

   ------- - - - - - - -

   I _____  .

3. _____

   ------- - - - - - - -

   _____ **see**  .

4. _____

   ------- - - - - - - -

   I _____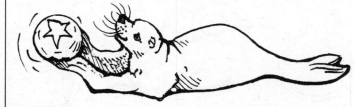

    .

THEME 2: Colors All Around
Week Two
High-Frequency Word *see*

60

Children
- read the sentences and write *I* or *see* to complete them
- mark the smile (yes) or the frown (no) to show whether the picture goes with the sentence

 Home Connection
I am learning to read the word *see*. Let me read this cartoon to you!

Name _____

1.

2.

3.

THEME 2: Colors All Around
Week Two *In the Big Blue Sea*
Making Predictions, Responding

Children
- predict what the child in each picture will do
- draw a picture of their prediction

 Home Connection
Let me tell you about the story
In the Big Blue Sea. Then I'll tell
you what the pictures I drew
show.

61

Name _____

Mm M m

THEME 2: Colors All Around
Week Two
Phonics: Initial Consonant _m_

Children
• write _Mm_ at the top
• name the pictures Mimi Mouse thinks about
• color and write _m_ beside pictures whose
  names begin with the sound for _m_

 Home Connection
Can you help me find some
things or pictures of things
whose names start with the
sound for _m_?

Name _____

I see

1.

_____

_____

I _____ .

2.

_____

_____

_____ see .

3.

_____

_____

I _____ .

4.

I see

Children
for 1, 2, and 3,
• read the sentence and write *I* or *see* to complete it
for 4,
• read the sentence and draw a picture to complete it

 Home Connection
Let me read these sentences to you. Then maybe we can draw other pictures that could finish sentence 4.

64 Just for fun, color all the hats! Name the colors you choose.

Name _____

1 **2** **3**

THEME 2: Colors All Around
Week Three *How the Birds Got Their Colors*
Sequence of Events

Children
• draw lines from 1, 2, and 3 to what happened first, next, and last in the story
• color the pictures

 Home Connection
Let me tell you what happened first, next, and last in a story called *How the Birds Got Their Colors*. I'll point to the pictures as I tell it.

65

Name _____

1.

2.

3.

THEME 2: Colors All Around
Week Three *How the Birds Got Their Colors*
Responding

Children
for 1 and 2,
• color the first picture and circle the picture beside it that shows what happens next
for 3,
• draw what happens first, next, and last in a story about how they would have rewarded the birds

 Home Connection
Maybe we can find other make-believe stories at the library that tell why some things are the way they are.

Name _____

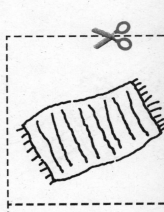

THEME 2: Colors All Around
Week Three
Phonemic Awareness: /r/

Children
- color all the pictures on pages 67 and 68 whose names start like *Reggie Rooster*
- cut and paste pictures for that sound in the boxes on page 68
- draw something else whose name starts with that sound

Home Connection
Let's name all the things on the front and back whose names start like *Reggie Rooster*.

67

Name _____

THEME 2: Colors All Around
Week Three
Phonemic Awareness: /r/

Name _____

R r   R _ _ _ _ _ _ _   r _ _ _ _ _ _ _

THEME 2: Colors All Around
Week Three
Phonics: Initial Consonant r

Children
• write *Rr* at the top
• name the pictures Reggie Rooster thinks about
• color and write *r* beside pictures whose names begin with the sound for *r*

 Home Connection
Let's look in some books for words that start with *r*. You can read the words to me, and I'll listen for the sound for *r*.

69

THEME 2: Colors All Around
Week Three *In the Big Blue Sea*
Making Predictions, Responding

Children
- choose a fish they would like to be; color it
- look at the pictures of places
- predict what they would see if they were a fish
- color that picture

Home Connection
Let me tell about the fish I colored and what I predicted it would see.

Name _____

1.

2.

THEME 2: Colors All Around
Week Three
Phonics: Initial Consonant _r_

Children
- draw lines from pictures whose names start with the sound for _r_ to _Rr_
- write _Rr_ and draw something else for that sound in the box with Reggie Rooster

 Home Connection
Let me tell you which picture names start with the sound for _r_. Then let's look for things at home whose names start with the sound for _r_.

71

Name _____

I see

1.

_____

- - - - - - - - - -

I _____ [chickens] .

2.

_____

- - - - - - - - - -

_____ see [rabbits] .

3.

_____

- - - - - - - - - -

I _____ [rings] .

 4.

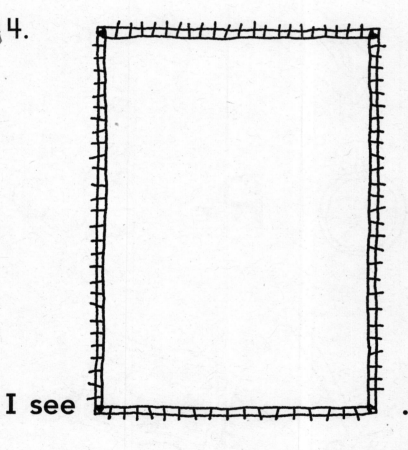

I see _____ .

THEME 2: Colors All Around
Week Three
High-Frequency Word Review _I, see_

Children
for 1, 2, and 3,
- read the sentence and write _I_ or _see_ to complete it

for 4,
- read the sentence and draw a picture to complete it

Home Connection
I am learning to read the words _I_ and _see_. Let me read this cartoon to you and tell you what I see.

72

Name _____

1.

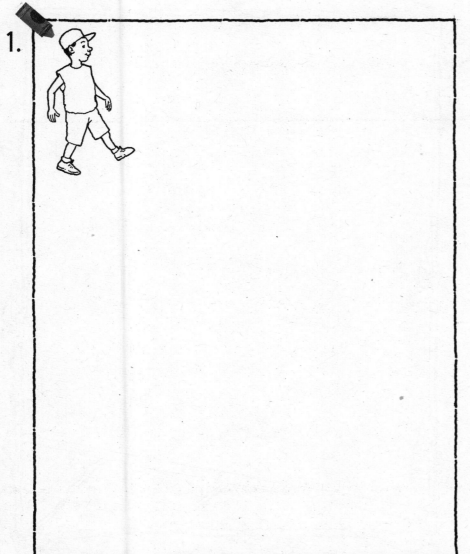

2.

THEME 3: We're a Family
Week One *Jonathan and His Mommy*
Characters/Setting

Children
1. draw the family member the boy in the story took a walk with
2. color pictures of things the story characters saw when they jumped, skipped, and danced through their neighborhood together

 Home Connection
Let me tell you about a story called *Jonathan and His Mommy* and what they saw when they took a walk.

73

Name _____

1.

2.

THEME 3: We're a Family
Week One *Jonathan and His Mommy*
Responding

Children

1. draw themselves on a neighborhood walk with one of their family members
2. draw what they might see on their walk

 Home Connection
Let me tell you about the pictures I drew. On our next walk, let's see what we see that Jonathan and his mommy saw.

Name _____

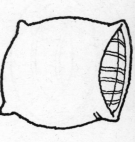

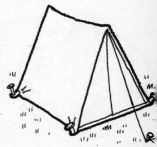

THEME 3: We're a Family
Week One
Phonemic Awareness: /t/

Children
- color all the pictures on pages 75 and 76 that start like *Tiggy Tiger*
- cut and paste the pictures for that sound in the boxes on page 76
- draw something else that starts with that sound

 Home Connection
Let's name the things on the front and back that start like *Tiggy Tiger*.

75

Name _____

Name _____

1.  **T t**

2.

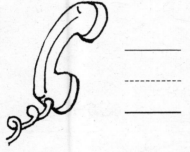

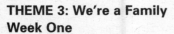

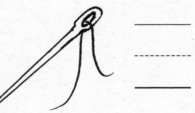
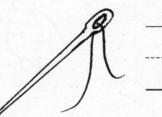

3.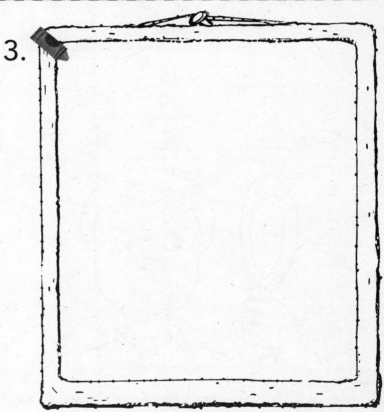

THEME 3: We're a Family
Week One
Phonics: Initial Consonant _t_

Children
- for 1 and 2, write _Tt_ beside the pictures whose names start like _Tiggy Tiger_
- for 3, draw a picture with two things whose names start with the sound for _t_

 Home Connection
Today we learned the letter _t_.
Let's look in an old newspaper
for pictures whose names begin
with the sound for _t_.

77

Name _____

1.

_____

See _____ 👀 ?

my

2.

_____

I see _____ 👃 .

3.

_____

I see _____ 👂 .

4.

_____

I see _____ 👄 .

THEME 3: We're a Family
Week One
High-Frequency Word *my*

78

Children
• read the sentences and write *my* to complete them
• draw the missing face parts to complete each picture

Home Connection
Let me read this cartoon to you. Then we can cut it apart, make a cover and put it together into a comic book.

Name _____

THEME 3: We're a Family
Week One *Tortillas and Lullabies*
Characters/Setting, Responding

Children
- circle the pictures that show characters a story might be about
- color the pictures that show places a story might tell about
- draw a line between each character and a place it might be

 Home Connection
Let's think of some other characters who could be in stories and draw places they might be.

Name _____

T t   T   t

12

THEME 3: We're a Family
Week One
Phonics: Initial Consonant *t*

80

Children
• write *Tt* at the top
• name the pictures Tiggy Tiger thinks about
• color and write *t* beside pictures whose names begin with the sound for *t*

Home Connection
Next time we watch TV together, let's look for things whose names start with the sound for *t*.

Name _____

I   see   my

1.

I _____ my  .

2.

_____ see my .

3.

I see _____ 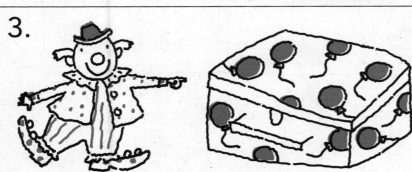 .

4.

I see my .

THEME 3: We're a Family
Week One
High-Frequency Words Review *I, see, my*

Children
• for 1, 2, and 3, read the sentences and write *I*, *see*, and *my* to complete them
• for 4, draw a picture to go with the sentence

Home Connection
Let me read these sentences to you. Then let's think of other spotted things a clown might tell about.

81

82   Just for fun, color the pictures of families. How many people are in each picture?

Name _____

THEME 3: We're a Family
Week Two *Goldilocks and the Three Bears*
Drawing Conclusions

Children
- color the pictures that give clues about which of the Three Bears will be the most unhappy when the bears get home
- draw a picture of that bear

Home Connection
Let me tell you about this picture. Which bear do you think will be most upset to see what Goldilocks has done?

83

1.

2.

3.

4.

THEME 3: We're a Family
Week Two *Goldilocks and the Three Bears*
Responding

Children
- for 1, 2, and 3, color the picture that shows the way they might have told the bears they were sorry if they had been Goldilocks
- for 4, draw another way Goldilocks might have apologized

 Home Connection
Let me tell you about these pictures and how I think Goldilocks should have told the bears she was sorry.

Name _____

THEME 3: We're a Family
Week Two
Phonemic Awareness: /b/

Children
• color all the pictures on pages 85 and 86 that start like *Benny Bear*
• cut and paste the pictures for that sound in the boxes on page 86
• draw something else that starts with that sound

 Home Connection
Let's name all the things on the front and back that start like *Benny Bear*.

Name _____

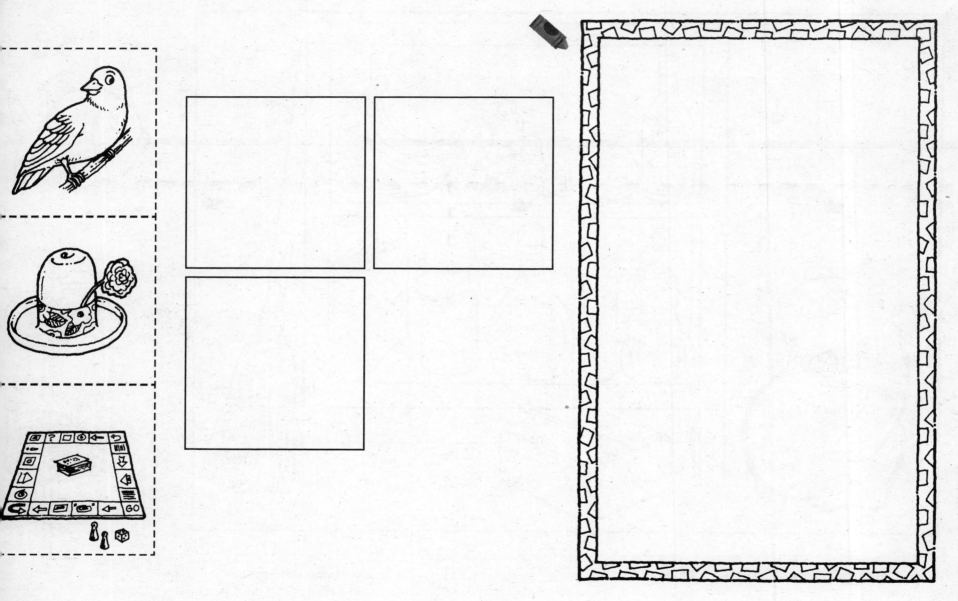

THEME 3: We're a Family
Week Two
Phonemic Awareness: /b/

Name _____

1. 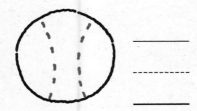 **Bb** B ___ b ___ 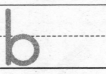 ___ ___

2.  ___

 ___

 ___

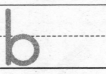 ___

 ___

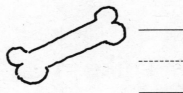 ___

 3.

THEME 3: We're a Family
Week Two
Phonics: Initial Consonant b

Children
- for 1 and 2, write *Bb* beside pictures whose names start like *Benny Bear*
- for 3, draw a picture with two things whose names start with *b*

 Home Connection
Let me tell you which pictures start with the sound for *b*. Then let's look for other things that start with the sound for *b*.

87

Name _____

like

1. _____
   - - - - - - - - - - - - - -
   _____

  .

4.

2. _____
   - - - - - - - - - - - - - -
   I _____

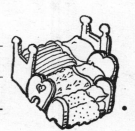
  .

3. _____
   - - - - - - - - - - - - - -
   _____

  .

I like

Children
• for 1, 2, and 3, read the sentences and write *like* to complete them
• for 4, read the sentence and draw a picture to complete it

 Home Connection
Let me read the sentences and pictures to you. Then I'll tell you about the picture I drew.

Name _____

1.

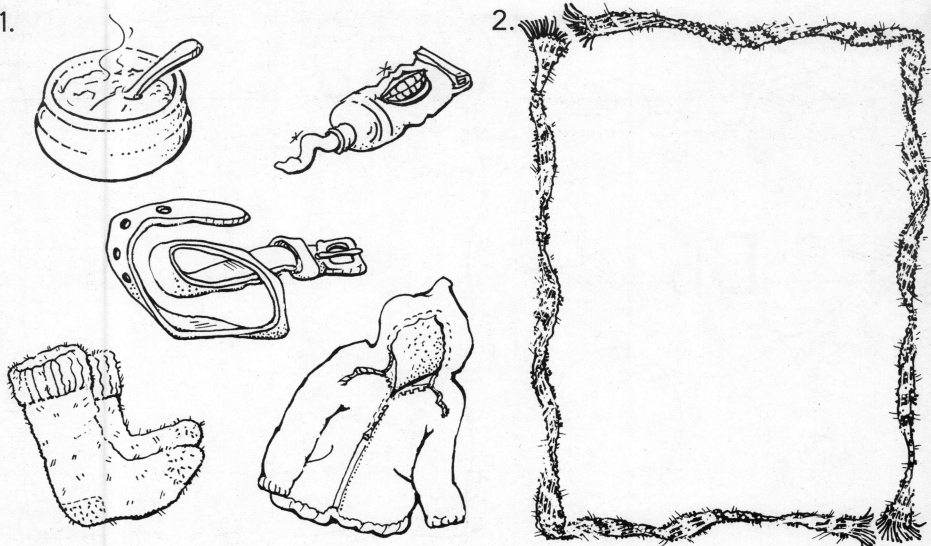

2.

THEME 3: We're a Family
Week Two *Shoes from Grandpa*
Drawing Conclusions, Responding

Children
1. color what else Jessie's family members might get her if she gets the jeans she asked for at the end of the story
2. draw some kind of clothing they might wish for as a birthday gift

 Home Connection
Let me tell you a story called *Shoes from Grandpa*. Then let's talk about who the members of our family are.

89

Name _____

1.

2.

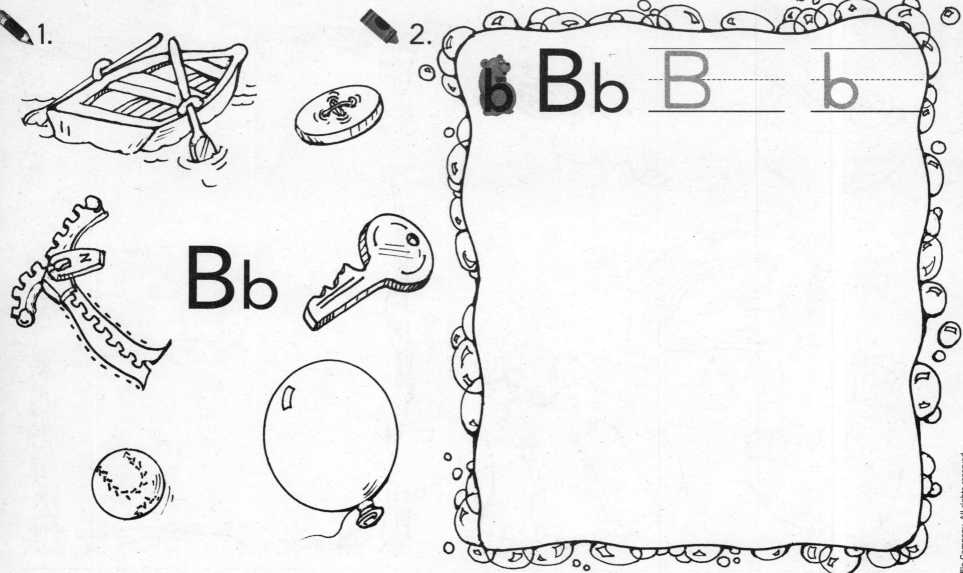

Bb

B   B   b

THEME 3: We're a Family
Week Two
Phonics: Initial Consonant _b_

Children
- draw lines from pictures whose names start with the sound for _b_ to _Bb_
- draw something else for that sound in the box with Benny Bear

Home Connection
Let me tell you about the picture I drew. Then let's look for more things whose names start with the sound for _b_.

Name _____

I like my

✏️ 1.

I _____

_____  .

_____ like  .

I _____ 🐟 .

🖍️ 2.

I like _____

THEME 3: We're a Family
Week Two
High-Frequency Words Review *like, my*

Children
1. read the sentences and write *I* and *like* to complete them
2. write *my* to finish the sentence and draw a picture of a pet they might like to have

 Home Connection
Let me read these sentences to you. Then you can help me write a list of things in my room that I like.

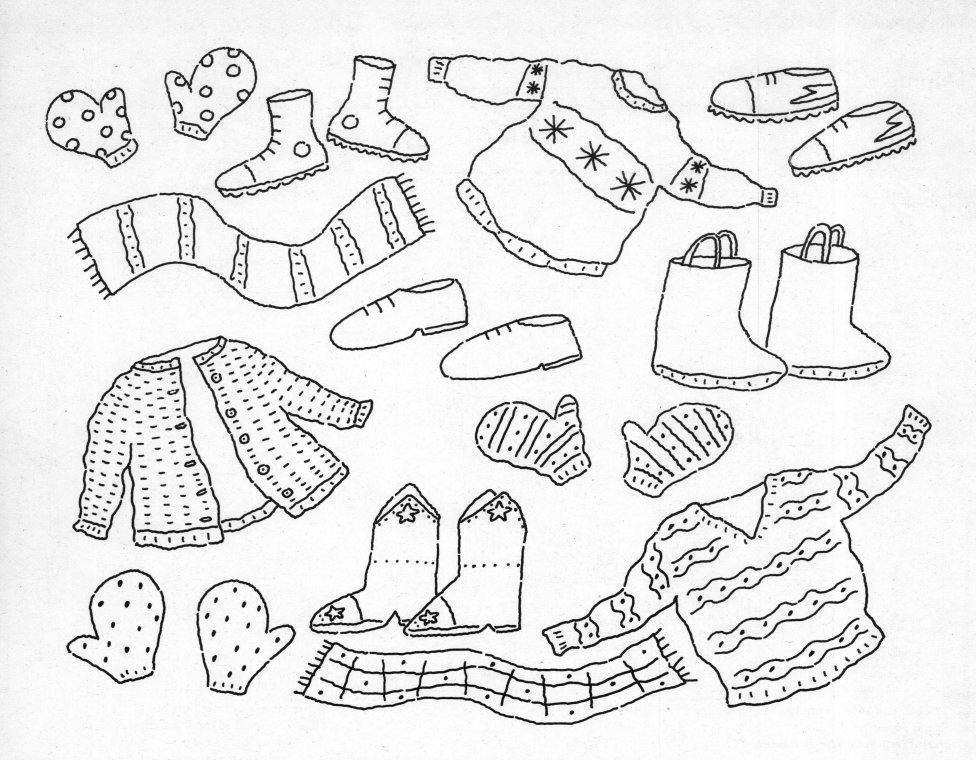

Just for fun, color the things to wear on your feet!

Name _____

THEME 3: We're a Family
Week Three *The Amazing Little Porridge Pot*
Comprehension, Drawing Conclusions

Children
- draw beside each picture what they think the woman must do to solve the problem she finds in that room

 Home Connection
Let me tell you about what the woman found when she came home and about the pictures I drew.

Name _____

THEME 3: We're a Family
Week Three *The Amazing Little Porridge Pot*
Responding

Children
• look at the pictures that show different endings for the story
• color the picture that shows the ending they might have chosen to write for the story

 Home Connection
If I had written the story, *The Amazing Little Porridge Pot*, I might have written a different ending for it. Let me tell you about it.

94

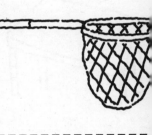

THEME 3: We're a Family
Week Three
Phonemic Awareness: /n/

Children
- color all the pictures on pages 95 and 96 that start like *Nyle Noodle*
- cut and paste pictures for that sound in the boxes on page 96
- draw something else that starts with that sound

Home Connection
Let's name all the things on the front and back that start like *Nyle Noodle*.

95

Name _____

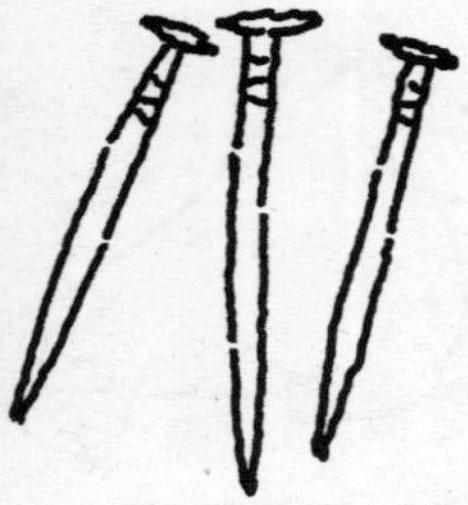

THEME 3: We're a Family
Week Three
Phonemic Awareness: /n/

Name _____

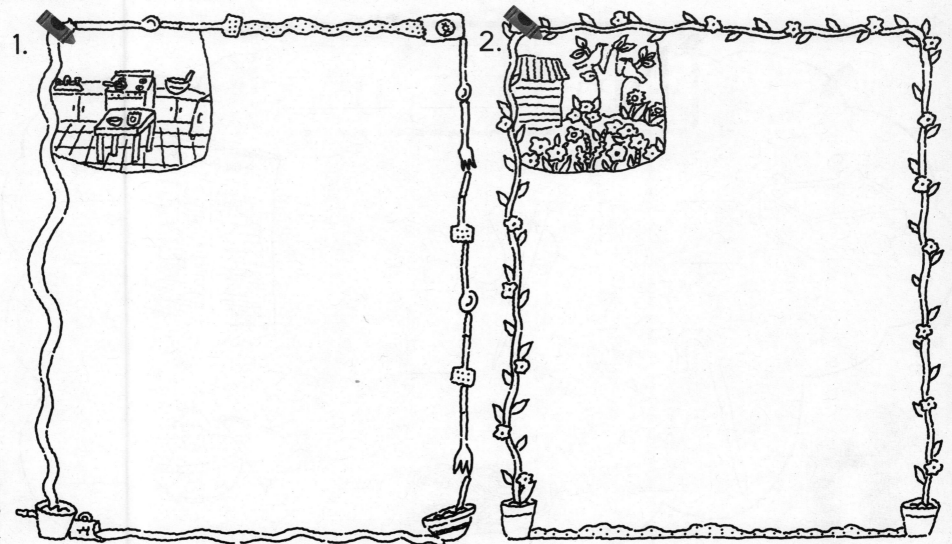

1.

2.

THEME 3: We're a Family
Week Three *Tortillas and Lullabies*
Character/Setting, Responding

Children

1. think about something one of the people in the story did in the kitchen and draw a picture of her doing that

2. think about something one of the people in the story did in the garden and draw a picture of her doing that

 Home Connection
Let me tell you the story we heard today called *Tortillas and Lullabies*. Then maybe we can look at pictures of my grandmothers and great-grandmothers.

97

Name _____

N n N n

THEME 3: We're a Family
Week Three
Phonics: Initial Consonant _n_

Children
- write _Nn_ at the top
- name the pictures Nyle Noodle thinks about
- color and write _n_ beside pictures whose names begin with the sound for _n_

Home Connection
Let's look in a newspaper for pictures of things that start like _Nyle Noodle_.

Name _____

like   my

1. **I like my**  .

2. **I like** _____  .

3. **I** _____ **my**  .

4. **I like** _____  .

THEME 3: We're a Family
Week Three
High-Frequency Words Review *my, like*

Children
• read the sentences and write *like* and *my* to complete them

 Home Connection
Let's write *like* and *my* on a piece of paper. Then I can make up sentences with these words and you can write my sentences.

Name _____

1.

2.

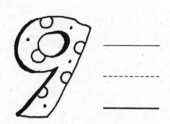

3.

THEME 3: We're a Family
Week Three
Phonics: Initial Consonant _n_

Children
- for 1 and 2, write _Nn_ beside the pictures whose names start like _Nyle Noodle_
- for 3, draw two things that start with the sound for _n_

Home Connection
Let me tell you about the things on the page that begin with the sound for _n_.

Name _____

1.

2.

n N n _____ N _____ n

THEME 3: We're a Family
Week Three
Phonics: Initial Consonant *n*

Children

1. draw lines from pictures whose names start with the sound for *n* to *Nn*

2. write *Nn* and draw something else for that sound in the box with Nyle Noodle

 Home Connection
Let me tell you about the picture I drew. Then let's look for more things whose names start with the sound for *n*.

Name _____

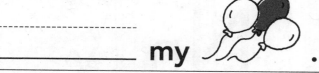

I   my   like   See

1.

See _____ .

2.

_____ **my**  .

3.

_____ **like my** .

4.

I _____ **my**  .

THEME 3: We're a Family
Week Three
High-Frequency Words Review _my, like, I, see_

Children
- read the sentences and write _I, my, like_ and _See_ to complete them
- draw a picture to go with sentences 2 and 4

 Home Connection
Let me read the sentences to you. Then we can cut apart the words at the top and use them with cut-out magazine words to make other sentences.

102

Name _____

1.

2.

3.

THEME 4: Friends Together
Week One _Friends at School_
Organization and Summarizing

Children

1. think about the friends in the story and color the pictures

2. draw something one group of friends did together in the story

3. color those things the friends played with in the story

 Home Connection

Today my teacher read us a story _Friends at School_. Let me tell it to you. I'll use the pictures to help me remember parts of it.

103

Name _____

THEME 4: Friends Together
Week One *Friends at School*
Responding

Children
- draw what they and a friend might do with each of the school-related things

 Home Connection
Ask me what kinds of things I like to do with my friends. What did you like to do with your friends at school when you were my age?

Name _____

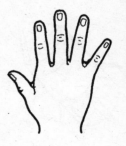

THEME 4: Friends Together
Week One
Phonemic Awareness: /h/

Children
- color all the pictures on pages 105 and 106 that start like *Hattie Horse*
- cut and paste pictures for that sound in the boxes on page 106
- draw something else that starts with that sound

 Home Connection
Let's name all the things on the front and the back that start like *Hattie Horse*.

105

Name _____

Name _____

1.  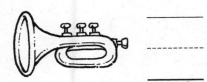 **Hh** H _____ h _____ _____  _____

2. 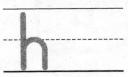 _____

 _____

 _____

 _____

 _____

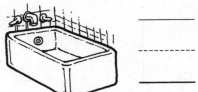 _____

3.

THEME 4: Friends Together
Week One
Phonics: Initial Consonant _h_

Children
• for 1 and 2, write _h_ beside the pictures whose names start like *Hattie Horse*
• for 3, draw a picture of two things whose names start with _h_

 Home Connection
Today we learned the letter _h_.
Help me find pictures in books of things that start like *Hattie Horse*.

Name _____

a

1. See _____ ⭐.
😊 ☹️

2. See _____ ☁️.
😊 ☹️

3. See _____ 🐰.
😊 ☹️

4. See _____

Children
For 1, 2, and 3
- read the sentences and write *a* to complete them
- mark yes (smile) or no (frown) to show whether the pictures go with the sentences
For 4, read the sentence and draw something they would like to see

Home Connection
Let me read these questions to you and we can see if you answer them the same way I did.

Name _____

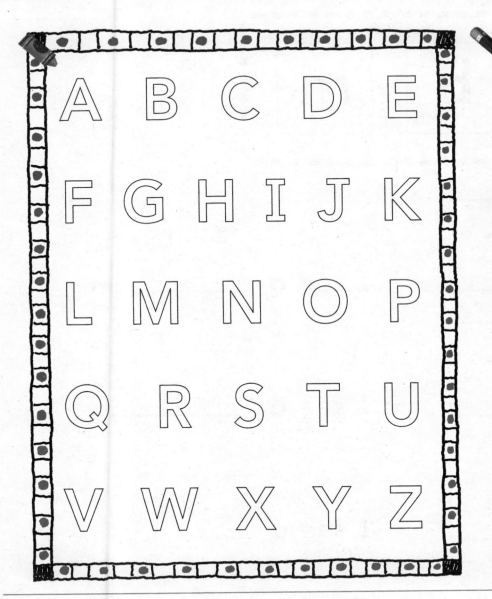

My name is

_____

- -

_____

THEME 4: Friends Together
Week One *Aaron and Gayla's Alphabet Book*
Text Organization & Summarizing, Responding

Children
- name the letters of the alphabet
- color the letter that begins their own name
- write their name on the line
- draw a picture of themselves

 Home Connection
Will you sing the ABC song
with me? We can point to the
letters as we sing.

109

Name _____

 a t

I see a _____ .

 a t

I see a _____ .

 a n

I see a _____ .

 THEME 4: Friends Together
Week One
Phonics: *h,* **Short** *a* **Words**

Children
- write letters to complete the picture names (*bat, hat, man*)
- write each word to complete the sentences

 Home Connection
Let's cut out the letter squares, mix them up, and build the words *hat, bat,* and *man* again.

Name _____

s	a	t
r	a	n
b	a	t

_____
- -
_____

_____
- -
_____

_____
- -
_____

_____
- -

A cat _____ .

_____
- - - - - - - - - - - - - - -

A fat rat _____ .

_____
- - - - - - - - - - - - - - -

I see Nat at _____ .

THEME 4: Friends Together
Week One
Phonics: Short *a* Words

Children
- add letters to build *sat*, *ran*, and *bat*
- write each word to complete the sentences

Home Connection
Would you like to listen to me read the words and sentences on this page? Then we can make up some other short *a* words.

Name _____

a   see   like

1. _____
   _____
   I see _____ cat I like.

2. _____
   I see a hat I _____.

3. _____
   I _____ a bat I like.

4. I see a _____

THEME 4: Friends Together
Week One
High-Frequency Words Review: *a, see, like*

Children
• for 1, 2, and 3 write *a, see,* or *like* to complete the sentences
• for 4, draw a picture to complete the sentence

Home Connection
Let me read these cartoons to you. Then we can cut them into four smaller pages and make a comic book and a cover for it.

Name _____

1.

2.

THEME 4: Friends Together
Week Two *The Lion and the Mouse*
Cause and Effect

Children
1. color what made the mouse afraid
2. color the picture that shows what its promise to the lion caused the mouse to do

 Home Connection
Let me tell you the story *The Lion and the Mouse*. Then you'll know what caused the mouse to chew a hole in the net.

113

Name _____

1.

2.

THEME 4: Friends Together
Week Two *The Lion and the Mouse*
Responding

Children

1. imagine they were the author of the story and draw a picture to show a different way the mouse might help the lion

2. draw a picture of a friend in need of help and how they might help that friend

 Home Connection

Today we heard a story called *The Lion and the Mouse*. Will you listen as I tell it to you? Then I'll tell you about the pictures I drew.

Name _____

THEME 4: Friends Together
Week Two
Phonemic Awareness: /v/

Children
- color all the pictures on pages 115 and 116 that start like *Vinny Volcano*
- cut and paste pictures for that sound in the boxes on page 116
- draw something else that starts with that sound

 Home Connection
I'll name the pictures on the front and back that start like *Vinny Volcano*. Then let's find things around the house that start with that sound.

Name _____

Name _____

✏️ **1.**

🖍️ **2.**

Vv   V   V   v

THEME 4: Friends Together
Week Two
Phonics: Initial Consonant _v_

Children

1. draw lines from pictures whose names begin with the sound for _v_ to the letters _Vv_

2. write _Vv_ at the top and complete the picture of the exploding volcano

 Home Connection
Today I finished this exploding volcano picture. Let me show it to you. Then I can tell you about the other pictures that begin with the sound for _v_.

Name _____

cat

to _____

bat

I like _____ see my cat.

I like _____ see a bat.

THEME 4: Friends Together
Week Two
High-Frequency Word: *to*

Children
- read the words that name the pictures and write *to*
- read the sentences and write *to* to complete them
- draw pictures to go with the sentences

 Home Connection
I can read these sentences to you. Then I'll tell you about the pictures I drew to go with the sentences.

Name _____

1.

2.

THEME 4: Friends Together
Week Two _My Dad and I_
Cause and Effect

Children

1. circle the pictures that show something the father and son in the story played together, because they are friends

2. draw a picture of something they themselves play with someone, because they are friends

Home Connection
We heard a story called _My Dad and I_ today. Let me tell it to you. Then I'll tell you about the picture I drew and why I drew it.

119

Name _____

vat hat van

See my _____ .

See my _____ .

See my _____ .

THEME 4: Friends Together
Week Two
Phonics: *v*, Short *a* Words

Children
- read the sentences and write the short *a* words to complete them
- mark the smile (yes) or the frown (no) to show whether the pictures go with the sentences

 Home Connection
Let me read the questions to you and tell you about my answers. Then will you help me make up more sentences with those words?

Name _____

s	m	v

	a	t

I like my _____ .

	a	n

See my _____ .

	a	t

A cat _____ .

THEME 4: Friends Together
Week Two
Phonics: Short *a* Words

Children
• write letters to complete the picture names (*mat, van, sat*)
• write each word to complete the sentences

 Home Connection
Let me read the sentences to you. Then we can cut out the letter squares, mix them up, and build the words *mat, van,* and *sat.*

121

to   a   My   like

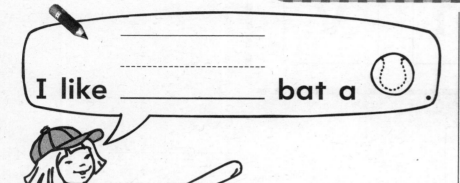

I like _____ bat a  .

_____ cat sat!

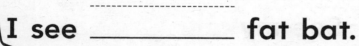

I see _____ fat bat.

I _____ my hat.

THEME 4: Friends Together
Week Two
High-Frequency Words Review: *to, a, my, like*

Children
• read the cartoons
• write *a*, *to*, *my*, and *like* to complete the sentences
• complete the last picture

Home Connection
Today I finished this cartoon. Let me read it to you. Then we can cut apart the four cartoon boxes, make a book with them, and read it to someone else.

Name _____

THEME 4: Friends Together
Week Three *Stone Soup*
Cause and Effect

Children
- think about the story *Stone Soup* and how the man tricked the villagers into making wonderful soup
- color those ingredients that caused the soup to become so tasty and add two more things that could be added to make it even better

 Home Connection
We heard the story *Stone Soup* today. Ask me to tell you about it. I can point to the pictures I colored as I tell that part of the story.

Name _____

THEME 4: Friends Together
Week Three *Stone Soup*
Responding

124

Children
- think about whether the stone had anything to do with making the soup tasty
- imagine how the story would be different if the man asked for help making some stone pizza instead
- draw their ideas

Home Connection
Let me tell you about my picture and the story I drew it for.

Name _____

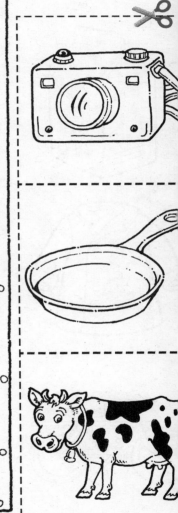

THEME 4: Friends Together
Week Three
Phonemic Awareness: /c/

Children
- color all the pictures on pages 125 and 126 that start like *Callie Cat*
- cut and paste pictures for that sound in the boxes on page 126
- draw something else that starts with that sound

Home Connection
Let's name all the things on the front and back that start like *Callie Cat.*

Name _____

THEME 4: Friends Together
Week Three
Phonemic Awareness: /c/

Name _____

A B C D E F _____
H I J K L M N
O P Q R S T
U V W X Y Z

A B _ D E F G
H I J K L M N
O P Q R S T
U V W X Y Z

A B C D E
F G H I J K
L M N O P
Q R S T U
V W X Y Z

THEME 4: Friends Together
Week Three *Aaron and Gayla's Alphabet Book*
Text Organization and Summarizing, Responding

Children
• write the letters missing from the alphabet
• play this game in pairs: one partner covers a letter with a coin or token, and the other tells what letter is covered

Home Connection
Today I learned to play "Hide the Letter." I can teach it to you.

127

Name _____

C c   C   c

THEME 4: Friends Together
Week Three
Phonics: Initial Consonant *c*

128

Children
- write *C c* at the top
- name the pictures *Callie Cat* thinks about
- color and write *c* beside pictures whose names begin with the sound for *c*

Home Connection
Today we learned the letter *c*. Can you help me find a few things around our house that start like *Callie Cat*?

Name _____

a to see

1. _____

I sat _____ see a 🐕 .

2. _____

I sat to _____ a 🦆 .

3. _____

I sat to see _____ 🐍 .

4. I sat to see a cat.

THEME 4: Friends Together
Week Three
High-Frequency Words Review: *a, to*

Children
• for 1, 2, and 3, read the cartoons, write *a*, *to*, and *see* to complete the sentences, and color the cartoons
• for 4, draw a cartoon to go with the sentence

 Home Connection
Listen while I read these cartoons to you. Then we can cut them apart to make a comic book.

129

Name _____

| cat | man | fat | sat |

See my fat _____ .

I see a _____ .

My _____ cat _____ .

**THEME 4: Friends Together
Week Three
Phonics: c, Short a Words**

130

Children
• write short *a* words to complete the sentences
• mark smile (yes) or frown (no) to show whether the picture goes with the sentence

 Home Connection
Let's write *cat*, *man*, *fat*, and *sat* and make up some more sentences using these words.

h	v	N

	a	t

I see _____ at bat.

	a	n

My _____ is tan.

	a	t

I like my _____ .

THEME 4: Friends Together
Week Three
Phonics: Short *a* Words

Children
• write *h*, *v*, or *N* to complete the words (*Nat*, *van*, *hat*)
• write each word to complete the sentences about the pictures

Home Connection
Can I read these sentences to you? Then we can cut out the letter squares, mix them up, and use them to build the words *Nat*, *van*, and *hat* again.

131

Name _____

Word box: **to   My   like   a**

1.

_____

_____ cat sat.

I _____ my cat.

2.

_____

See _____ rat?

3.

_____

My cat ran _____ see a
rat.

4.

Children
• for 1, 2, and 3, read the sentences and write words to complete them
• for 4, draw a picture to show how the story might end

Home Connection
I can read these sentences to you. Then I'll tell you about the picture I made that shows how the story ends.

Name _____

1.

2.

THEME 5: Let's Count!
Week One: *Benny's Pennies*
Categorize & Classify

Children
1. draw presents Benny bought for his family
2. draw presents Benny bought for his family's pets

 Home Connection
Ask me to tell you about a story
called *Benny's Pennies*.

133

Name _____

1.

2.

THEME 5: Let's Count!
Week One *Benny's Pennies*
Responding

Children

1. draw things they would buy members of their own families and the pennies it might take to buy each

2. draw things they would buy for a friend and the pennies it might take to buy each

Home Connection
Can you help me think of some good gifts for our family?

134

Name _____

THEME 5: Let's Count!
Week One
Phonemic Awareness: /p/

Children
- color all the pictures on pages 135–136 that start like *Pippa Pig*
- cut and paste pictures for that sound in the boxes on page 136, then draw something else that starts with that sound

Home Connection
Let's name all the things on the front and the back that start like *Pippa Pig*.

135

Name _____

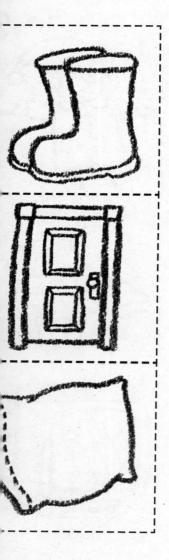

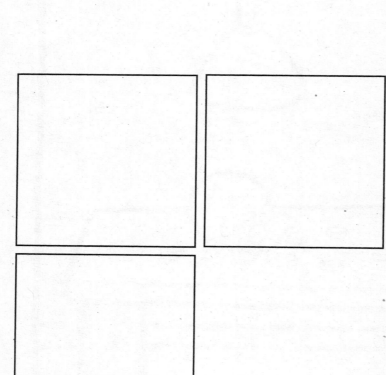

Name _____

1.

2.

3.

THEME 5: Let's Count!
Week One
Phonics: Initial Consonant _p_

Children
- for 1 and 2, color and write _p_ beside the pictures whose names start like _Pippa Pig_
- for 3, draw pictures of two _p_ things

 Home Connection
Today we learned the letter _p_.
Help me find pictures of things
that start with the sound for _p_.

137

Name _____

and

 1. _____

See my _____ cat?

☺ ☹

2. _____

See my _____ cat?

☺ ☹

3. _____

See my _____ cat?

☺ ☹

4. _____

See my _____ cat.

Children
- read the sentences and write *and* to complete them
- mark smile (yes) or frown (no) to answer the questions
- draw the last picture

 Home Connection
Let me read these sentences to you.

Name _____

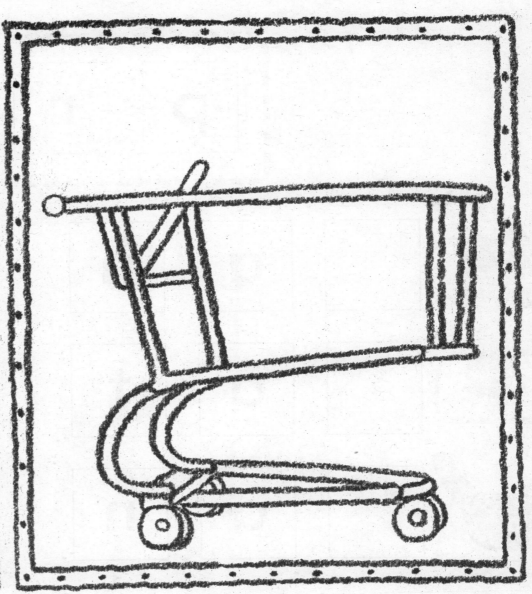

THEME 5: Let's Count!
Week One _Feast for 10_
Categorize and Classify, Responding

Children
• color things they saw in the story _Feast for 10_
• draw foods in the cart they would buy for their own family's meal

 Home Connection
Today we heard a story called _Feast for 10_. Ask me to tell you about it.

139

Name _____

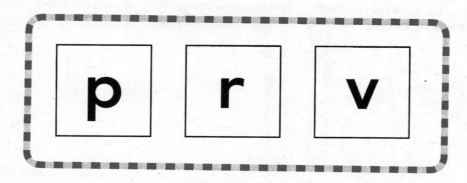

p   r   v

   [ ]   a   n

I see a bat _____.

   [ ]   a   t

I see a _____ mat.

   [ ]   a   n

I see a cat _____.

 THEME 5: Let's Count!
Week One
Phonics: *p,* **Short** *a* **Words**

140

Children
- write letters to complete the picture names
  (*pan, rat,* or *van*)
- write each word to complete the sentences

 Home Connection
I can read these sentences. We
can cut out the letter squares and
build the words again. Then, we
can make up some other silly hats.

Name _____

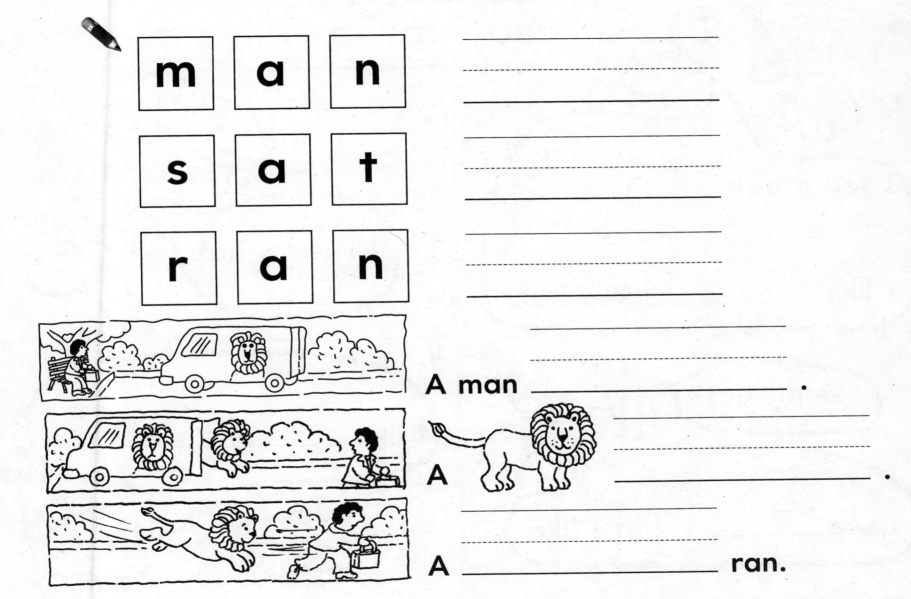

| m a n |
| s a t |
| r a n |

_____

_____

_____

_____

_____

A man _____ .

A _____ .

A _____ **ran.**

THEME 5: Let's Count!
Week One
Phonics: Short *a* Words

Children
• add letters to short *a* to build the words *man*, *sat*, *ran*
• write these words to complete the sentences

 Home Connection
Please listen to me read these words and sentences.

Name _____

| and | to | a |

1.

I see a hat, _____

_____

I like _____ see a hat.

2.

I like my hat.

3.

See my hat?

I see _____ hat I like.

4.

I like _____ see a hat.

Children
• read the sentences in the cartoon and write
and, to, or _a_ to complete them

Home Connection
I'll read this cartoon to you. Then
we can cut it apart to make a
comic book.

Name _____

THEME 5: Let's Count!
Week Two *Counting Noodles*
Beginning/Middle/End

Children

1. think about the beginning of the story
2. finish the picture to show the middle of it
3. draw what the Noodles kept on doing at the end of the story

Home Connection
Let me tell you the story, *Counting Noodles*. Then we can count the Noodle family.

143

Name _____

THEME 5: Let's Count!
Week Two *Counting Noodles*
Responding

Children
- think about a new story they might tell about the Noodles on a farm
- draw their ideas for their new story

Home Connection
This is a picture for a story about the Noodles on a farm. Let me tell you about it.

Name _____

THEME 5: Let's Count!
Week Two
Phonemic Awareness: /g/

Children
- color all the pictures on pages 145 and 146 that start like *Gertie Goose*
- cut and paste the pictures for that sound in the boxes on page 146, then draw something else that starts with that sound

Home Connection
Let's name all the things on the front and the back that start like *Gertie Goose.*

145

Name _____

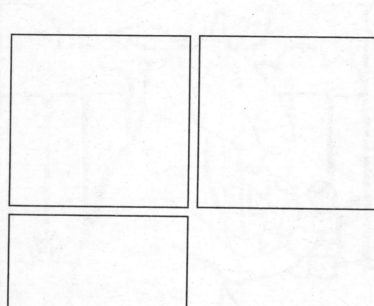

THEME 5: Let's Count!
Week Two
Phonemic Awareness: /g/

Name _____

1.

2. g G g

Gg

Children
1. draw lines from pictures whose names start with the sound for g to the letters Gg
2. write Gg on the lines and draw something else that starts with the sound for g.

 Home Connection
Today we learned the letter g. Help me find magazine pictures whose names start with the sound for g.

147

Name _____

van

go

bat

_____

A van can _____ to a .

A bat can _____ to a .

Children
• read the sentences and write *go* to complete them
• complete the pictures for each sentence

Home Connection
I can read these sentences to you. Let's write *go*, *van*, and *bat*, then we can make up other sentences using these words.

Name _____

THEME 5: Let's Count!
Week Two *Ten Little Puppies*
Beginning/Middle/End, Responding

Children

1. count the puppies and draw more to show how many the boy had at the beginning

2. draw what one of the puppies did in the middle of the story

 Home Connection
Let me tell you the story *Ten Little Puppies*. Then I'll tell you about the pictures.

149

Name _____

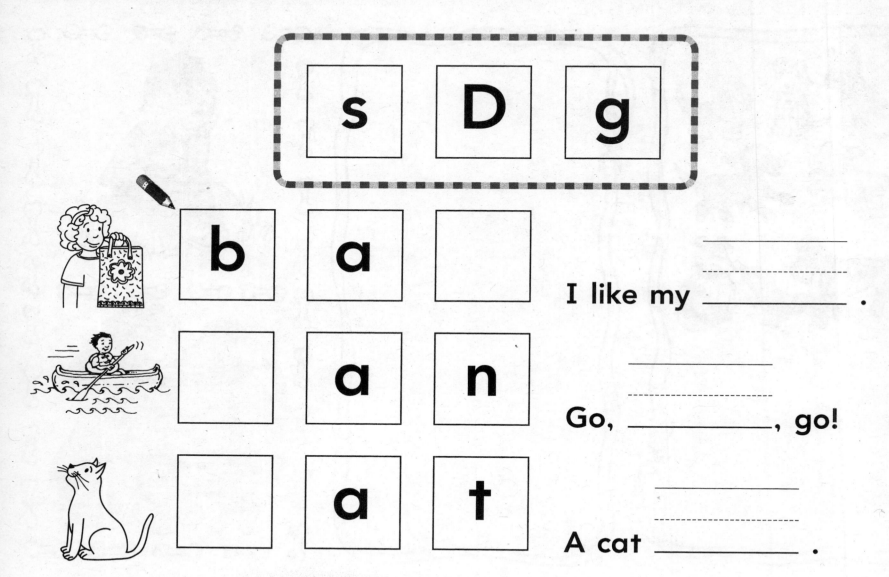

s	D	g

b a

I like my _____ .

a n

Go, _____, go!

a t

A cat _____ .

THEME 5: Let's Count!
Week Two
Phonics: _g_, Short _a_ Words

150

Children
- write letters to complete the picture names _bag_, _Dan_, and _sat_
- write each word to finish the sentences

Home Connection
Let's cut out the letter squares, I'll read the sentences, then we can build _bag_, _Dan_, and _sat_ again.

Name _____

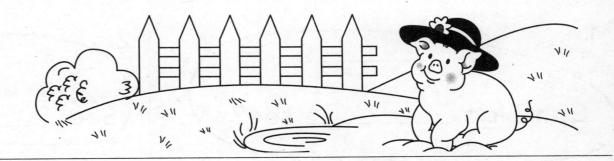
man hat ran

_____

See my _ _ _ _ _ _ _ _ .

_____

My cat _ _ _ _ _ _ _ _ .

_____

A _ _ _ _ _ _ _ _ **ran.**

THEME 5: Let's Count!
Week Two
Phonics: Short *a* Words

Children
- read the sentences and write short *a* words to complete them
- mark the smile (yes) or the frown (no) to show whether the pictures go with the sentences

 Home Connection
I'll read these sentences. Then we can write *hat*, *ran* and *man* on a paper and make up more sentences using them.

151

Name _____

my and go

1. Can I go _____ see?

2. See _____ van go?

3. Can I _____ and see?

4. I see a hat.

THEME 5: Let's Count!
Week Two
High-Frequency Words Review *go, and*

152

Children
- read the cartoon and write *my, and, go* to complete what the children are saying
- complete the picture for 4 so it goes with the sentence

Home Connection
Today I finished this cartoon. We could cut these four cartoon boxes apart and make them into a comic book.

Name _____

1.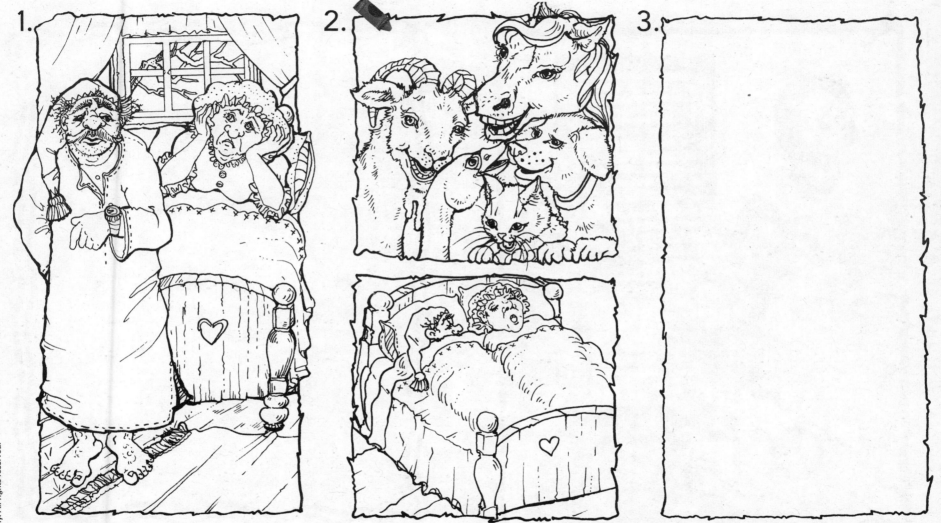

2.

3.

THEME 5: Let's Count!
Week Three _Peace and Quiet_
Beginning/Middle/End

Children
1. think about what happened in the beginning
2. color the picture that shows what happened in the middle
3. draw what the man and woman did at the end

 Home Connection
Let me tell you the story _Peace and Quiet_. I'll use the pictures to help me remember what happened at the beginning, in the middle, and at the end.

153

Name _____

1.

2.

THEME 5: Let's Count!
Week Three *Peace and Quiet*
Responding

154

Children
1. circle the things that are making noises
2. draw a picture of what they might do to make the noisy things quiet

 Home Connection
Let's take a walk around our house and find some things that make noises that might keep us awake.

Name _____

THEME 5: Let's Count!
Week Three
Phonemic Awareness: /f/

Children
- color all the pictures on 155 and 156 that start like *Fifi Fish*
- cut and paste the pictures for that sound in the boxes on page 156
- draw something else that starts with that sound

 Home Connection
Let's name the things on the front and back that start like *Fifi Fish*.

155

Name _____

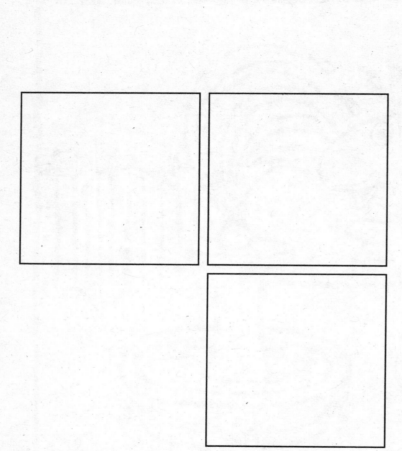

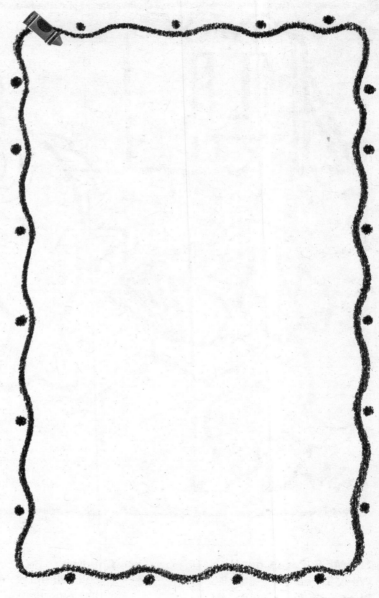

Name _____

1.

2.

3.

THEME 5: Let's Count!
Week Three _Feast for 10_
Categorize & Classify, Responding

Children

1. draw lines from things to eat you might get at the market to the cart
2. draw lines from things you would set the table with to the table
3. draw what you and your family might eat

Home Connection
Let me tell you about this page and the special meal I drew.

157

Name _____

F f F -------------- f --------------

THEME 5: Let's Count!
Week Three
Phonics: Initial Consonant _f_

Children

- write _Ff_ at the top
- name the pictures _Fifi Fish_ thinks about
- color and write _f_ beside pictures whose names begin with the sound for _f_

Home Connection
Today we learned the letter _f_. Help me find things around the house that start with the sound for _f_.

Name _____

I   and   go

1.

I sat _____ sat.

2.

Can I _____ ?

3.

_____ sat and sat.

4.

I can go!

THEME 5: Let's Count!
Week Three
High-Frequency Words Review *and, go*

Children
- Read the cartoon and write *I*, *and*, and *go* to complete what the fish says
- complete the picture for 4 to show how the fish will go

Home Connection
I can read this cartoon to you. What do you think comes to get the fish?

Name _____

f	a	n

v	a	n

c	a	t

_____

_____

_____

_____

_____

I can _____ .

A _____ can go.

A _____ sat.

THEME 5: Let's Count!
Week Three
Phonics: f, Short a Words

160

Children
• blend and write the words *fan*, *van*, and *cat*
• write each word to finish the sentences

Home Connection
We could cut the sentences into
strips, and draw a picture to go
with each.

Name _____

s	f	p

| | a | n | I see a _____. |

| | a | t | A cat _____. |

| | a | n | See my _____ hat. |

Children
• Add letters to write the words *fan*, *sat* and *pan*.
• Write words to complete the sentences

 Home Connection
Let me read the sentences to you. Then we can cut out the letter squares, mix them up, and make the words again.

161

Name _____

and go a to

1. _____

Can a cat _____ ?

☺ ☹

2. _____

Can _____ go?

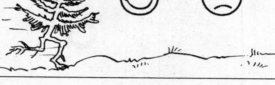

☺ ☹

3. _____

A man _____ a cat can go.

☺ ☹

4.

I see a man and a .

THEME 5: Let's Count!
Week Three
High-Frequency Words Review *and, go, a, to*

Children
For 1, 2, 3,
• read the questions and write *and*, *go*, *a*, and *to* to complete them
• mark smile (yes) or frown (no) to show whether the pictures answer the questions

For 4, read the sentence and draw a picture to go with it

Home Connection
Let me read these sentences to you. Then we can check to make sure the pictures go with the questions.

162

Name _____

THEME 6: Sunshine and Raindrops
Week One *Chicken Soup with Rice*
Fantasy/Realism

Children
- color the pictures that show what might happen in a make-believe story but not in real life
- draw a picture of something that could happen in real life

 Home Connection
Let me tell you about the story *Chicken Soup with Rice* and why I colored the pictures that I did.

Name _____

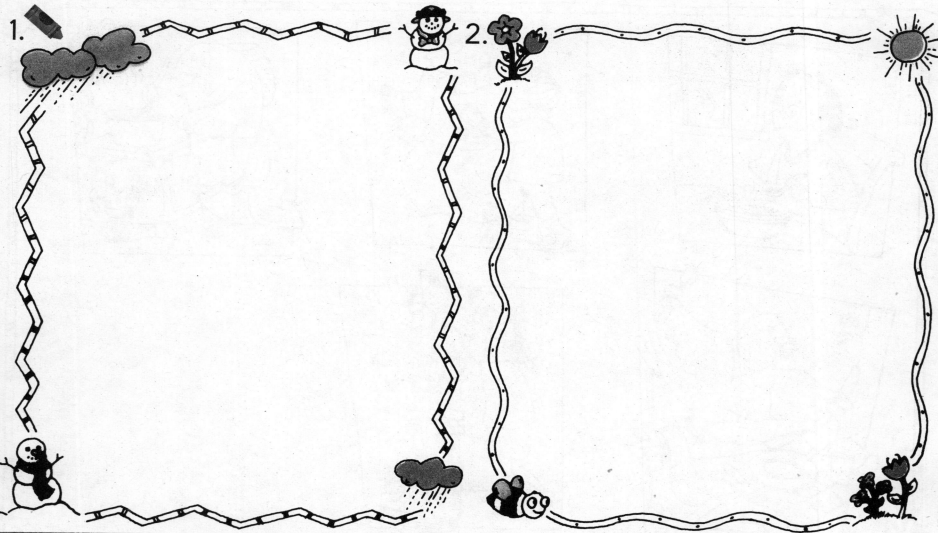

1.

2.

THEME 6: Sunshine and Raindrops
Week One *Chicken Soup with Rice*
Responding

Children

think of a favorite food they would like to eat all year long, in any kind of weather. Then they

1. draw themselves eating that food in hot weather

2. draw themselves eating that food in cold weather

 Home Connection

Let me tell you about some of the silly things a boy did in different months of the year in *Chicken Soup with Rice*. Then I'll tell you about the pictures I drew about a favorite food of mine.

Name _____

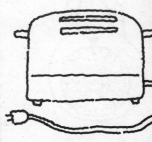

THEME 6: Sunshine and Raindrops
Week One
Phonemic Awareness: /l/

Children

- color all the pictures on pages 165 and 166 that start like *Larry Lion*
- cut and paste pictures for that sound in the boxes on page 166
- draw something else that starts with that sound

 Home Connection
Let's name all the things on the front and back that start like *Larry Lion*.

165

Name _____

Name _____

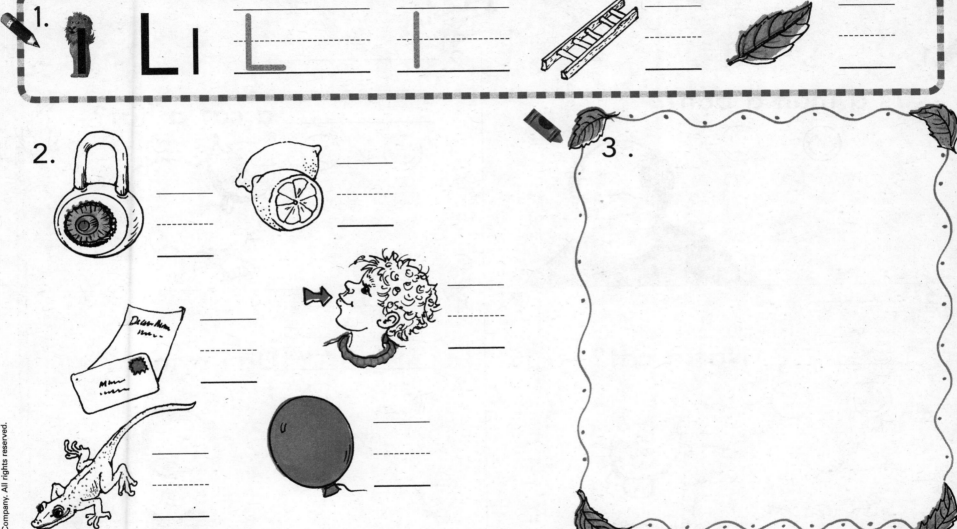

1. Ll L l

2.

3.

THEME 6: Sunshine and Raindrops
Week One
Phonics: Initial Consonant *l*

Children
- for 1 and 2, write *l* beside the pictures whose names start like *Larry Lion*
- for 3, draw two things whose names start with *l*

 Home Connection
Would you help me find things in our house that start with the sound for *l*? Then we can make a list of what we find.

Name _____

Is

1.

Is a man a pan?

2. _____

a cat a hat?

3. _____

Nat a cat?

4. _____

Dan a man?

THEME 6: Sunshine and Raindrops
Week One
High-Frequency Word: *is*

Children
- read the questions and look at the pictures
- write *Is* to complete 2, 3, and 4
- mark yes (smile) or no (frown) to show their answers to the questions

 Home Connection
Ask me to read these questions to you. Then we can take turns asking other questions like these about things in this room.

168

Name _____

1.

2.

THEME 6: Sunshine and Raindrops
Week One *What Will the Weather Be Like Today?*
Fantasy/Realism, Responding

Children
1. color the picture that shows something that probably wouldn't happen in that kind of weather
2. draw something they themselves would do in the kind of weather shown

 Home Connection
My teacher read a book to us called *What Will the Weather Be Like Today?* Let me tell you what I learned about weather from it and about the pictures I colored and drew.

Name _____

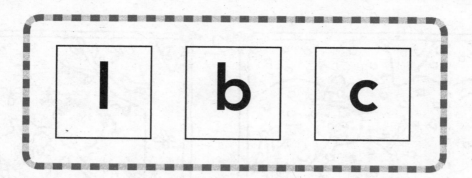

l	b	c

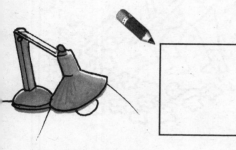

	i	t
	a	n
	i	t

My 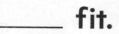 is _____.

_____
A cat _____ fit.

_____
A rat _____ my .

THEME 6: Sunshine and Raindrops
Week One
Phonics: *l*, Short *i* and Short *a* Words

Children
- write the letters to complete the picture names (*lit, can,* and *bit*)
- write each word to complete the sentences

 Home Connection
We can cut out the letter squares on this page, mix them up and unscramble them to build the words *lit, can,* and *bit* again.

170

Name _____

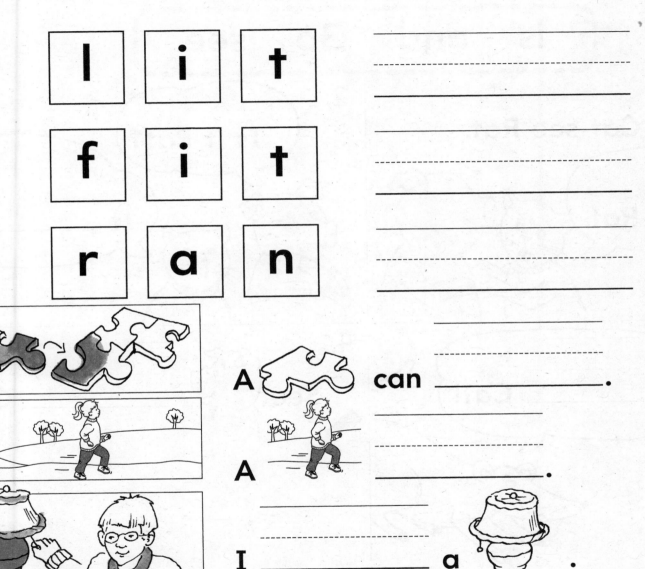

l	i	t
f	i	t
r	a	n

_____
- -
_____

_____
- -
_____

_____
- -
_____

A can _____.

A _____.

I _____ a _____ .

THEME 6: Sunshine and Raindrops
Week One
Phonics: Short _i_ and Short _a_ Words

Children
- blend and write the words *lit*, *fit*, and *ran*
- write these words to complete the sentences that go with the pictures

Home Connection
Ask me to read the sentences I finished to you. Then we can make up a silly sentence using the words I wrote.

171

Name _____

is   and   Go   see

1. and Cat see Rat.

I _____ Rat.

2. Is it Rat?

It _____ Rat.

3. Go _____! _____ Cat!

4. See _____ Cat go!

THEME 6: Sunshine and Raindrops
Week One
High-Frequency Words Review *is, and, go*

Children
• read the sentences in the cartoons and write words to complete them
• draw who Pig and Cat are running away from

Home Connection
Let me read this cartoon to you. Then we can draw and write some more cartoon pictures together of something Pig, Cat, and Rat do.

172

Name _____

1.

2.

Theme 6: Sunshine and Raindrops
Week Two *The Sun and the Wind*
Plot

Children
1. draw what the man did when the wind blew harder and what he did when the sun got hotter
2. color the picture of the winner of the contest between the sun and the wind

Home Connection
Let me tell you about what happened in a story I heard today called *The Sun and the Wind.*

173

Name _____

1.

2.

Children
1. draw what they themselves would wear outside on a hot and sunny day and what they might do that day
2. draw what they themselves would wear outside on a very windy day and what they might do that day

 Home Connection
Let me tell you about the pictures I drew of myself in different kinds of weather.

Name _____

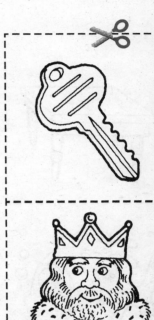

THEME 6: Sunshine and Raindrops
Week Two
Phonemic Awareness: /k/

Children
- color all the pictures on pages 175 and 176 that start like *Keeley Kangaroo*
- cut and paste pictures for that sound in the boxes on page 176
- draw something else that starts with that sound

Home Connection
Let's name all the things on the front and back that start like *Keeley Kangaroo.*

Name _____

THEME 6: Sunshine and Raindrops
Week Two
Phonemic Awareness: /k/

Name _____

1.

K k

2.

k K k K ----- k

THEME 6: Sunshine and Raindrops
Week Two
Phonics: Initial Consonant *k*

Children
- draw lines from the pictures whose names start with the sound for *k*, to *Kk*
- write *Kk* and draw something else for that sound in the box with Keely Kangaroo

 Home Connection
Let's look in story books to find some words that start with *k*. Every time we find one, you can read it and I'll write a *k* on a list so we can count how many words we find.

Name _____

cat

Here   here

rat

_____

_____ is a cat I

can see.

I can see a rat

_____

_____

_____.

THEME 6: Sunshine and Raindrops
Week Two
High-Frequency Word *here*

Children
• read the sentences and write *here* or *Here* to complete them
• draw a picture to go with each sentence

 Home Connection
Ask me to read these sentences to you. Then I'll tell you about the pictures I drew to go with them.

Name _____

THEME 6: Sunshine and Raindrops
Week Two *All to Build a Snowman*
Plot, Responding

Children
1. think about what happened in the story as the children built their snowman
2. draw something funny that happened before they finished
3. draw things they themselves would have added to the snowman if they had been there to help build it

 Home Connection
Let me tell you about the story *All to Build a Snowman*. It's about some funny things that happen when two children build a snowman.

179

Name _____

| l | m | k |

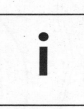
[ ] | i | t

A 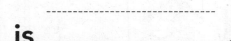 is _____ .

[ ] | i | t

I see a _____ .

[ ] | a | n

A _____ can hit a .

 THEME 6: Sunshine and Raindrops
Week Two
Phonics: *k,* Short *i* and Short *a* Words

Children
• write letters to complete the picture names (*lit, kit,* and *man*)
• write each word to finish the sentences

 Home Connection
Let me read the sentences I finished with the words *lit, kit,* and *man*. Then let's think of other sentences for these words. Will you write them for me?

180

Name _____

fit   man   kit

Is it a _____?

😊   ☹️

Can it _____?

😊   ☹️

Can a _____ sit?

😊   ☹️

THEME 6: Sunshine and Raindrops
Week Two
Phonics: Short *i* and Short *a* Words

Children
- read the questions and write short *i* and short *a* words to complete them
- mark the smile (yes) or the frown (no) to show whether the picture answers the question

 Home Connection
I can read these sentences to you! Then we can write the letters on separate scraps of paper and build the words again.

181

Name _____

> # Here   is   and   go

1. _____

Here _____ my cat.

2. _____

_____ is my .

3. _____

See my cat _____ to a

 4. _____

See my dog _____ my

cat go!

 THEME 6: Sunshine and Raindrops
Week Two
High-Frequency Words Review: *here, is,*
and, go

Children
• read the sentences and write *Here*, *is*, *and*, and *go*
  to complete them
• complete the picture in box 4 to go with the
  sentence

Home Connection
Let me read you the sentences I
finished and tell you about my
picture.

Name _____

Theme 6: Sunshine and Raindrops
Week Three *The Woodcutter's Cap*
Fantasy/Realism

Children
1. color the animals that crawled into the cap in the story
2. draw a line from the animals they colored to the homes where these animals would live in real life

 Home Connection
Let me tell you the make-believe story *The Woodcutter's Cap*. Then I'll tell you why this story could never happen in real life.

183

Name _____

1.

2.

**THEME 6: Sunshine and Raindrops
Week Three** *The Woodcutter's Cap*
Responding

Children

1. think about and draw what would have happened if more animals had tried to squeeze into the cap before the bee came

2. think about and draw what would have happened if the man had found his cap when all the animals were still in it

🏠 **Home Connection**
I drew some pictures that show what might have happened in the story if some parts of it had been different. Listen and I'll tell you about my pictures and my ideas.

184

Name _____

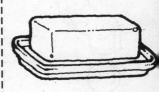

THEME 6: Sunshine and Raindrops
Week Three
Phonemic Awareness: /qu/

Children
- color all the pictures on pages 185 and 186 that start like *Queenie Queen*
- cut and paste the pictures for that sound in the boxes on page 186
- draw something else that starts with that sound

Home Connection
Let's name all the things on the front and back that start like *Queenie Queen*.

185

Name _____

THEME 6: Sunshine and Raindrops
Week Three
Phonemic Awareness: */qu/*

Name _____

1.

q Qu qu _____ Qu _____ qu _____ ? _____

2.

3.

THEME 6: Sunshine and Raindrops
Week Three
Phonics: Initial Consonant *qu*

Children
- for 1 and 2, write *qu* beside the pictures whose names start like *Queenie Queen*
- for 3, draw a picture of something else whose name starts with *qu*

Home Connection
Ask me to tell you about the pictures I wrote *qu* beside and about the picture I drew.

Name _____

Is   here

1. _____
_ _ _ _ _ _ _ _ _ _ _
_____ my cat here?

2. _____
_ _ _ _ _ _ _ _ _ _
Is my cat _____ ?

3. _____
_ _ _ _ _ _ _ _ _ _ _
_____ my cat here?

4. Here is my cat!

THEME 6: Sunshine and Raindrops
Week Three
High-Frequency Words Review *is, here*

Children
- read the questions and write *Is* and *here* to complete them
- read the last sentence and draw the cat in the place where the child found it

Home Connection
I finished the lines in this short story. Let me read it to you and tell you about the place the cat was hiding.

188

Name _____

1.

2.

THEME 6: Sunshine and Raindrops
Week Three *All to Build a Snowman*
Plot, Responding

Children
1. color the pictures that show something that happened in the story
2. draw two more things that they remember happened in the story

Home Connection
We heard a story today called *All to Build a Snowman*. Ask me to tell it to you. I can point to the pictures as I tell that part.

189

Name _____

  i   t

Can I _____ and sit?

   a   t

A cat _____ .

   i   t

Can Rat _____ ?

THEME 6: Sunshine and Raindrops
Week Three
Phonics: _qu_, Short _i_ and Short _a_ Words

190

Children
- write letters to complete the words (_quit, sat, fit_)
- write each word to finish the sentences

 Home Connection
There aren't very many words that start with _qu_. Help me look in books for some and you can read me the ones we find.

Name _____

| ran | sit | lit |

The fox ran.
☺ ☹

_____ a _____.
☺ ☹

can _____.
☺ ☹

THEME 6: Sunshine and Raindrops
Week Three
Phonics: Short *i* and Short *a* Words

Children
- read the sentences and write the words to complete them
- mark the smile (yes) or the frown (no) to show whether the sentence goes with the picture

 Home Connection
I've learned to read the words *ran*, *sit*, and *lit*. Let me read these sentences to you, then we can make up some silly rhymes with those words.

191

Name _____

```
is   Here   and   go
```

1. _____

I like to _____ here.

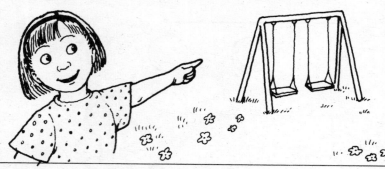

2. -------------

My cat _____ I like to go here.

3. _____

My cat _____ here.

4. _____

_____ is my cat!

THEME 6: Sunshine and Raindrops
Week Three
High-Frequency Words Review *is,*
here, and, go

Children
• write *go, and, is,* and *Here* to complete what the cartoon character says
• draw the place the child wants the cat to go

Home Connection
Ask me to read the sentences in the speech balloons to you. Then we can think of other places the cat and child might like to go.

Name _____

1.

2.

THEME 7: Wheels Go Around
Week One *Wheels Around*
Text Organization & Summarizing

Children

1. color the things with wheels and tell how wheels help those things do their jobs

2. draw something else that has wheels that they'd like to ride in

Home Connection
I colored some things with wheels that my teacher read about today. Ask me how wheels help these things do their jobs.

193

Name _____

1.

2.

**THEME 7: Wheels Go Around
Week One** *Wheels Around*
Responding

Children
1. draw a picture on the side of the big truck to show what it is carrying
2. draw a picture to show where the big truck might be taking its load

 Home Connection
Next time we ride somewhere, we can watch for big trucks. Ask me what I'd haul if I had a truck.

Name _____

THEME 7: Wheels Go Around
Week One
Phonemic Awareness: /d/

Children

- color all the pictures on pages 195 and 196 that start like *Dudley Duck*
- cut and paste pictures for that sound in the boxes on page 196
- draw something else that starts with that sound

 Home Connection
Let's name all the things on the front and back that start like *Dudley Duck*.

195

Name _____

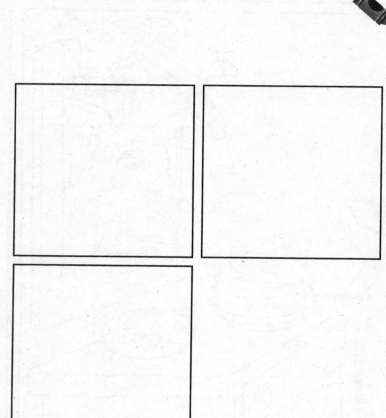

Name _____

1.  d D d D ___ d ___ 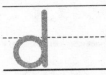 ___ ___

2.

3.

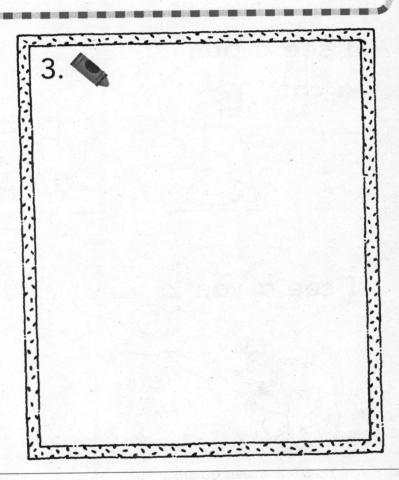

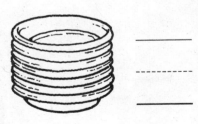

THEME 7: Wheels Go Around
Week One
Phonics: Initial Consonant *d*

Children

- for 1 and 2, practice writing *Dd* and then write *d* beside the pictures whose names start like *Dudley Duck*
- for 3, draw two things whose names begin with *d*

 Home Connection
Next time we watch TV together, let's see how many things beginning with *d* we can find. Would you write what we find?

197

Name _____

for

1. _____

I see a pan _____
a cat.

2. _____

I see a mat and a hat

_____

_____ a man.

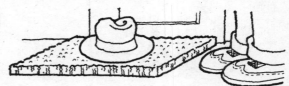

3. _____

I see a van _____ Nan.

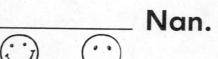

4. _____

I see a hat _____ Nan.

**THEME 7: Wheels Go Around
Week One
High-Frequency Word *for***

Children
- for 1, 2, and 3, read the sentences and write the word *for* on the lines
- mark the smile (yes) or the frown (no) to show whether the picture goes with the sentence
- for 4, draw a hat for Nan and write the word *for*

Home Connection
I am learning to read the word *for*. Let me read these sentences to you. Then we could make up some more about Nan.

198

Name _____

THEME 7: Wheels Go Around
Week One *The Wheels on the Bus*
Organization & Summarizing, Responding

Children
- for 1–6, cross out things that didn't happen on the bus in the story
- for the empty box, draw something else that did happen in the story

 Home Connection
I'll tell you what happened in the story *The Wheels on the Bus*. It's a song too, so if you know it, we can sing it together.

Name _____

k	p	d

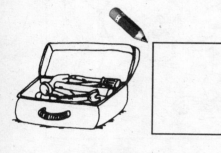

	i	t

Here is a _____ .

	i	g

A man can _____ .

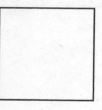

	i	g

Is the _____ here?

THEME 7: Wheels Go Around
Week One
Phonics: *d*, **Short** *i* **Words**

200

Children
- write the letters to complete the words *kit*, *dig*, *pig*
- write each word to complete the sentences that go with the pictures

Home Connection
Let's cut out the letter squares on this page, mix them up, and unscramble them to build the words *pig*, *dig*, and *kit* again.

Name _____

d	i	g
b	i	g
f	i	t

_____
_____
_____
_____
_____

Can Pat and Nat _____ in the van?

I like my _____ pig.

Dan and Nan can _____ .

THEME 7: Wheels Go Around
Week One
Phonics: Short *i* Words

Children
• blend and write the words *dig*, *big*, and *fit*
• write these words to complete the sentences that describe the pictures

Home Connection
Please listen to me read these sentences. Then we can make up more sentences using the same words.

Name _____

| for | is | Here |

1.

Here is a hat _____ Cat.

2.

Here _____ a fan for Cat.

3.

_____ is a mat for Cat.

4. Cat likes her hat, fan, and mat.

Children
• for 1, 2, and 3, write *for*, *is*, and *Here* to complete what the cartoon characters say
• for 4, draw a picture of Cat's mat, hat, and fan

Home Connection
Today I finished this cartoon.
Ask me to read it to you.

Name _____

1.

2.

THEME 7: Wheels Go Around
Week Two *The Little Engine That Could*
Cause and Effect

Children
1. think about what made the good little boys and girls happy at the end of the story and draw a picture to show that
2. draw something else they think would make the children happy

 Home Connection
Ask me to tell you about the picture I drew that shows why the children were happy at the end of the story *The Little Engine That Could*.

203

Name _____

THEME 7: Wheels Go Around
Week Two *The Little Engine That Could*
Responding

Children
- think about the Little Engine in the story who tried very hard to pull a big load over the mountain
- draw a picture of something they themselves tried very hard to do

 Home Connection
Ask me to tell you the story *The Little Engine That Could.* Then I'll tell you about something I tried very hard to do — just like the Little Engine in the story.

Name _____

THEME 7: Wheels Go Around
Week Two
Phonemic Awareness: /z/

Children
- color all the pictures on pages 205 and 206 that start like *Zelda Zebra*
- cut and paste pictures for that sound in the boxes on page 206
- draw something else that starts with that sound

Home Connection
Let's name all the things on the front and back that start like *Zelda Zebra*.

205

Name _____

Name _____

1.

2.

Z z Z z Z z

THEME 7: Wheels Go Around
Week Two
Phonics: Initial Consonant z

Children

1. draw lines from pictures whose names start with the sound for z to the Zz

2. write Zz and draw something else for that sound in the box with *Zelda Zebra*

 Home Connection
Let me tell you about the pictures I colored for the letter z and about the picture I drew. Then maybe you can help me write the name *Zelda Zebra*.

207

Name _____

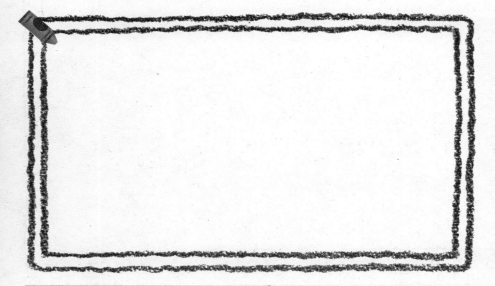

have
———————————

———————————

_____

I _____ to sit here.

_____

I _____ to hit it.

_____

I _____ a pan.

_____

I _____ a cat.

Children
• practice writing *have* on the lines at the top
• read the sentences above the boxes and write *have* to complete them
• choose and circle one sentence for each box
• draw a picture to go with it

Home Connection
Let me read these sentences to you! I drew pictures to go with two of the sentences. Let me tell you about them.

Name _____

1.

2.

3.

THEME 7: Wheels Go Around
Week Two *Vroom, Chugga, Vroom-Vroom*
Cause and Effect, Responding

Children
- think what problem each of the race cars is having and what might have caused the problem
- draw their ideas for the cause of the problems shown in 1, 2, and 3

Home Connection
Let me tell you about the story *Vroom, Chugga, Vroom-Vroom*. It's about a car race. All the cars had numbers. Have you ever been to or watched a car race? Tell me about it.

209

Name _____

Zig   bit   dig

1. _____

Here is my pig _____ .

2. _____

Zig Pig can _____ .

3. _____

My pig is a _____ fat.

Children
• read the sentences and write words to complete them
• mark the smile (yes) or the frown (no) to show whether the picture goes with the sentence beside it.

 Home Connection
Let me read these sentences to you! Then will you help me write the letters Z, i, b, d, p, t and g on separate scraps of paper? We can build words with them.

Z   p   s

[ ]   i   g

My cat _____ can dig.

[ ]   i   t

My cat can _____ .

[ ]   i   g

My cat and my _____ like to sit.

THEME 7: Wheels Go Around
Week Two
Phonics: Short *i* Words

Children
• write letters to complete the words that go with the pictures (*Zig, sit, pig*)
• write each word to finish the sentences

 Home Connection
Let me read you the sentences I finished with the words *Zig*, *sit*, and *pig*. Then let's think of other sentences for these words. Will you write them for me?

Name _____

1. _____
   I _____ a big fig.

2. _____
   Is it _____ Pig?

3. _____
   It _____ for Pig and
   Cat.

4. _____
   _____ is a big fig.
   A big fig

THEME 7: Wheels Go Around
Week Two
High-Frequency Words Review *have, for,*
is, here

212

Children
- read the speech balloons
- write a word from the box to complete what the characters are saying
- color the pictures

Home Connection
Let me read this cartoon to you. Then maybe you can read a newspaper cartoon to me.

Name _____

THEME 7: Wheels Go Around
Week Three *Mr. Gumpy's Motor Car*
Making Predictions

Children
- think about what is happening in the pictures and predict what will happen to the man, his car, and the rabbits
- draw their predictions in the box under each picture

 Home Connection
Let me tell you about the pictures I drew to show what I thought would happen next. Then let's talk about what else might happen for each picture.

213

Name _____

1.

2.

THEME 7: Wheels Go Around
Week Three *Mr. Gumpy's Motor Car*
Responding

Children
1. think about what they would draw for the cover of the book *Mr. Gumpy's Motor Car* if they were the artist and draw it
2. draw a picture of themselves in the car when they're grown-up enough to drive

 Home Connection
Let me tell you about *Mr. Gumpy's Motor Car*, a funny story that my teacher read to us. Ask me to tell you about the pictures I drew.

Name _____

THEME 7: Wheels Go Around
Week Three
Phonemic Awareness Review: /d/, /z/

Children
for each row,
- color the Alphafriend and two things whose names begin like the Alphafriend *Dudley Duck* or *Zelda Zebra*
- draw something else that starts with the same sound

Home Connection
Today I listened for words that start like *Dudley Duck* and *Zelda Zebra*. Ask me to tell you about the Alphafriends on this page and the pictures I colored.

215

Name _____

THEME 7: Wheels Go Around
Week Three
Phonemic Awareness Review: /d/, /z/

Children
- find and color two pictures that begin like *Dudley Duck*
- find and circle two pictures that begin like *Zelda Zebra*

Home Connection
Let's play a game. I'll look in a picture book for things whose names start like *Dudley Duck* and you can look for things that start like *Zelda Zebra*.

216

Name _____

THEME 7: Wheels Go Around
Week Three
Phonics Review: Initial Consonants *d, z*

Children
- use a yellow crayon to draw around *Dudley Duck* and to color all the pictures whose names begin with the sound for *d*
- use a blue crayon to draw around *Zelda Zebra* and to color all the pictures whose names begin with the sound for *z*
- write *d* beside yellow pictures and *z* beside blue pictures

 Home Connection
Today I colored pictures of things whose names begin with the sounds for *z* and *d*. Let me tell you about the blue and yellow pictures.

217

Name _____

for   have

1. _____

I _____ a hat for Nan.

2. _____

I have a bat _____ Nan.

3. _____

I _____ a van for Nan.

4. _____

I have a cat _____ Nan.

THEME 7: Wheels Go Around
Week Three
High-Frequency Words Review *for, have*

218

Children
• read the sentences and write *for* and *have* to complete them
• draw a picture to go with sentence 4

Home Connection
Today I wrote words and drew a picture to finish this short story. Let me read it to you.

Name _____

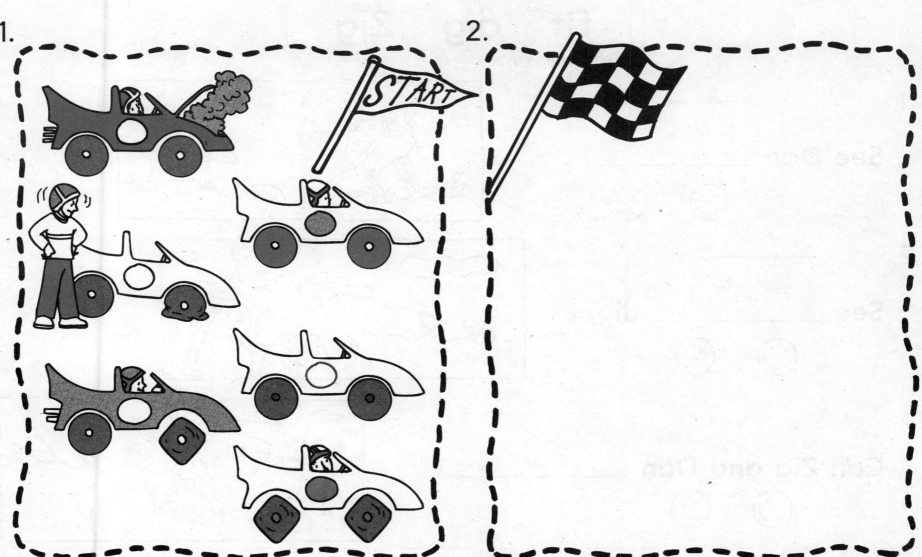

1.

2.

43180-T07W2-219A

THEME 7: Wheels Go Around
Week Three *Vroom, Chugga, Vroom-Vroom*
Making Predictions, Responding

Children

1. think about the troubles some of the race cars had in the story and color all the cars they think have a chance to win the race

2. draw a picture of the one car they predict will win

 Home Connection
Let me tell you why I thought the car I drew would be the winner of this race. Which one do you think might win? Why?

Name _____

fit   dig   Zig

1. _____ .

   See Dan _____ .

   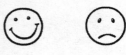

2. _____

   See _____ dig.

3. _____

   Can Zig and Dan _____ ?

THEME 7: Wheels Go Around
Week Three
Phonics: Short *i* Words

Children
- read the sentences and write words with short *i* to complete them
- mark the smile (yes) or the frown (no) to show whether the pictures go with the sentences

Home Connection
Let me read these sentences to you! Then will you help me write the letters Z, *i*, *d*, *b*, *f*, *g* and *t* on separate scraps of paper? Then we can see how many words we can build with them.

Name _____

b   Z   c

 i   g

Here is a _____ rig.

 a   n

A big rig _____ dig.

   i   g

_____ can get a big rig to dig.

THEME 7: Wheels Go Around
Week Three
Phonics: Short *i* and Short *a* Words

Children
• write the letters to complete the words *big*, *can*, and *Zig*
• write each word to complete the sentences that go with the pictures

 Home Connection
Let's look in a book together to find other words that end like *big* and *dig*. When we find them, would you help me read them?

221

Name _____

| have | for | is | Here |

1. _____

I have a hat _____
a man. ☺ ☹

2. _____

Here _____ a hat for
a . ☺ ☹

3. _____

I _____ a hat for a .
☺ ☹

4. _____

_____ is a hat I like.

Children
• for 1, 2, and 3, read the sentences and write words to complete them,
• mark the smile (yes) or frown (no) to show whether the sentences go with the pictures
• for 4, read the sentence and draw a hat they like

Home Connection
I wrote *have, for, is,* and *here* to finish the sentences. Let me read them to you, and tell you about my picture.

Name _____

1.

2.

THEME 8: Down on the Farm
Week One *The Story of Half-Chicken*
Fantasy/Realism

Children
for each box,
- decide which pictures show things that could really happen and which show things that could never happen in real life
- color the two pictures of things that could really happen

Home Connection
Ask me to tell you about these pictures. I'll tell you why I think the ones I didn't color are make-believe and could never happen in real life.

223

Name _____

1.

2.

3.

THEME 8: Down on the Farm
Week One *The Story of Half-Chicken*
Responding

Children

1. draw a picture of themselves meeting Half-Chicken on his way to the palace

2. draw a picture of Half-Chicken helping them in some way

3. draw a picture of something they would do to help Half-Chicken

 Home Connection
Let me tell you a story I heard today about a special chicken. He was called Half-Chicken. Then I'll tell you about the pictures I drew.

224

Name

1.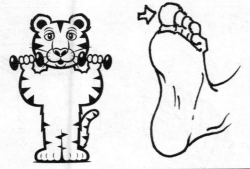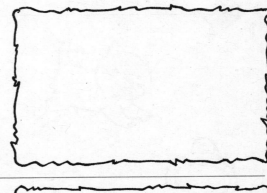

2.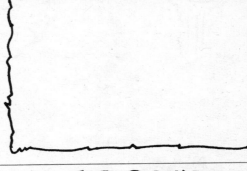

3.

THEME 8: Down on the Farm
Week One
Phonemic Awareness Review: /t/, /k/, /n/

Children
for each row,
- color the Alphafriend and two pictures whose names start like that Alphafriend's name
- draw something else whose name starts with the same sound

 Home Connection
Let me tell you about these Alphafriends and the pictures I colored and drew in each row.

Name _____

1.

2.

3.

THEME 8: Down on the Farm
Week One
Phonemic Awareness Review: /t/, /k/, /n/

Children
for each box,
• name the Alphafriend and the pictures
• color the pictures that have the same beginning sound as the Alphafriend
• draw lines to connect the pictures they colored with the Alphafriend

 Home Connection
Let's find magazine pictures whose names start like *Tiggy Tiger*, *Keely Kangaroo*, and *Nyle Noodle*.

226

Name _____

 **T** t _____  **k** **K** k _____  **n** **N** n _____

 _____

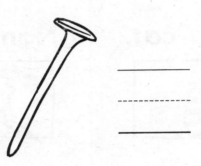 _____

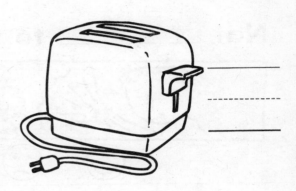 _____

 _____

 _____

 _____

THEME 8: Down on the Farm
Week One
Phonics Review: Initial Consonants t, k, n

Children
- name each Alphafriend and letters at the top
- write the letters *Tt, Kk, Nn*
- color the pictures and write the letter for the sound they hear at the beginning of each picture

 Home Connection
Let's see how many things we can find that begin with the sounds for *t, k,* or *n*. Will you write down what we find? Then I'll check to make sure they start with one of these letters.

227

Name _____

said

1.

_____

- - - - - - - - - - - - - -

Nat _____ to fan a cat.

😊 ☹️

2.

_____

- - - - - - - - - - - - - -

Nan _____ to fan a pig.

😊 ☹️

3.

_____

- - - - - - - - - - - - - -

Dan _____ to fan a rat.

😊 ☹️

4.

_____

- - - - - - - - - - - - - -

I _____, "Fan a rat?"

THEME 8: Down on the Farm
Week One
High-Frequency Word *said*

Children
- write the word *said* to complete each sentence
- read the sentences
- mark the smile (yes) or the frown (no) to tell whether the picture goes with the sentence

 Home Connection
I'm learning to read the word *said*. Let me read this cartoon to you.

228

Name

1.

2.

3.

4.

THEME 8: Down on the Farm
Week One *Cows in the Kitchen*
Fantasy/Realism, Responding

Children
for each box,
- decide which picture shows something silly that real cows, ducks, pigs, and chickens couldn't do in real life and color that picture

 Home Connection
Let me tell you about some farm animals that caused trouble in the story *Cows in the Kitchen*. Then we can make up some more parts for the story.

Name _____

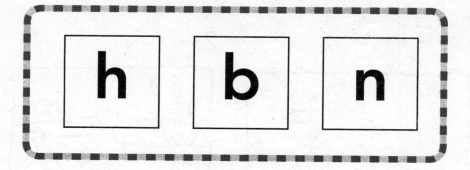

 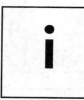

My cat is _____ .

My pot is _____ .

My pot is _____ **for a cat.**

 **THEME 8: Down on the Farm**
Week One
Phonics: *n*, Short *o* and Short *i* Words

230

Children
- write letters to complete the picture names *big*, *hot*, and *not*
- read the sentences and write the words to complete them

 Home Connection
Let's cut out the letter squares on this page, mix them up, and unscramble them. Then we can make the words *big*, *hot*, and *not* again.

Name _____

d	o	t
b	i	g
n	o	t

_____
_____
_____
_____
_____
_____
_____

I like a _____ to dot.

I can _____ hit it.

Here is a _____ pot.

THEME 8: Down on the Farm
Week One
Phonics: Short *o* and Short *i* Words

Children
• blend and write the words *dot*, *not*, *big*
• read the sentences about the pictures and write words to complete them

Home Connection
Would you like to help me read these sentences? Then we can make up other sentences using *dot*, *not*, and *big*.

231

Name _____

said   for   have

1.

Is a hat _____ Dan here?

2.

Dan _____, "I like a big hat."

3.

See a hat _____ Dan.

4.

I _____ a hat for Dan.

THEME 8: Down on the Farm
Week One
High-Frequency Words Review *said, for, have*

232

Children
- write the words to complete the sentences
- draw Dan's hat on the cat

Home Connection
Ask me to read this cartoon to you. Then I'll tell you about the hat for Dan that I drew.

Name _____

THEME 8: Down on the Farm
Week Two *The Enormous Turnip*
Noting Important Details

Children
- color who came to help when the grandfather called
- color who came to help when the grand-daughter called
- draw a picture of who came last to help pull up the turnip

 Home Connection
We heard a story called *The Enormous Turnip*. Do you know this story? Let me tell you who was in it and what happened.

233

Name _____

1.

2.

THEME 8: Down on the Farm
Week Two *The Enormous Turnip*
Responding

234

Children

- think about how the story would have been different (1) if no one had been around to help the farmer pull up the big turnip or (2) if the turnip hadn't been very big at all
- draw their ideas

Home Connection
Ask me to tell you about the pictures I drew that show my ideas for two different stories about pulling up a turnip.

Name _____

THEME 8: Down on the Farm
Week Two
Phonemic Awareness: /x/ in Final Position

Children
- color all the pictures on pages 235 and 236 that end in the sound they hear in *Mr. X-Ray*
- cut and paste the pictures for that sound in the boxes on page 236
- draw a picture of something else that ends with that sound

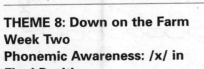

Home Connection
Today I listened for words that end with the sound I can hear in *Mr. X-Ray*. Let me tell you what they are.

235

Name _____

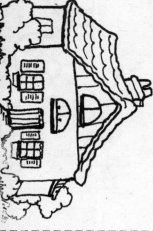

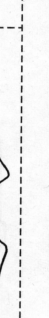

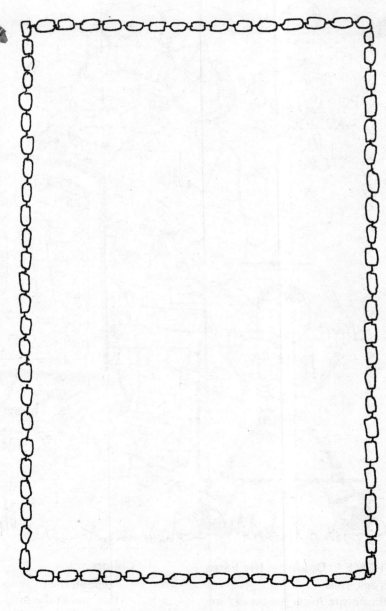

Name _____

1.

6

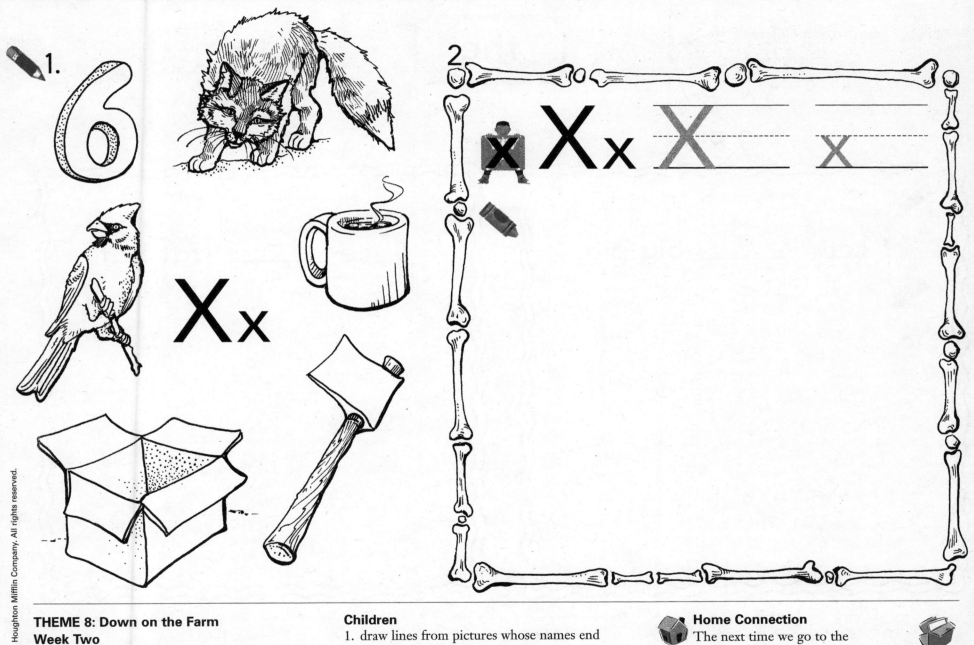

Xx

2

x Xx X x

THEME 8: Down on the Farm
Week Two
Phonics: *x* in final position

Children
1. draw lines from pictures whose names end with the sound for *x* to the *Xx*
2. write *Xx* and draw something else that ends with that sound in the box with *Mr. X-Ray*

 Home Connection
The next time we go to the library, let's find a book with pictures of x-rays in it.

237

Name _____

big pig

the

fat bat

_____
- - - - - - - - - - - - -
I see _____ big pig.

_____
- - - - - - - - - - - - -
I see _____ fat bat.

THEME 8: Down on the Farm
Week Two
High-Frequency Word *the*

Children
- read the word and the sentences
- write the word to complete the sentences
- draw a picture for each sentence

 Home Connection
Let me read these sentences to
you and tell you about the
pictures I drew for them.

Name _____

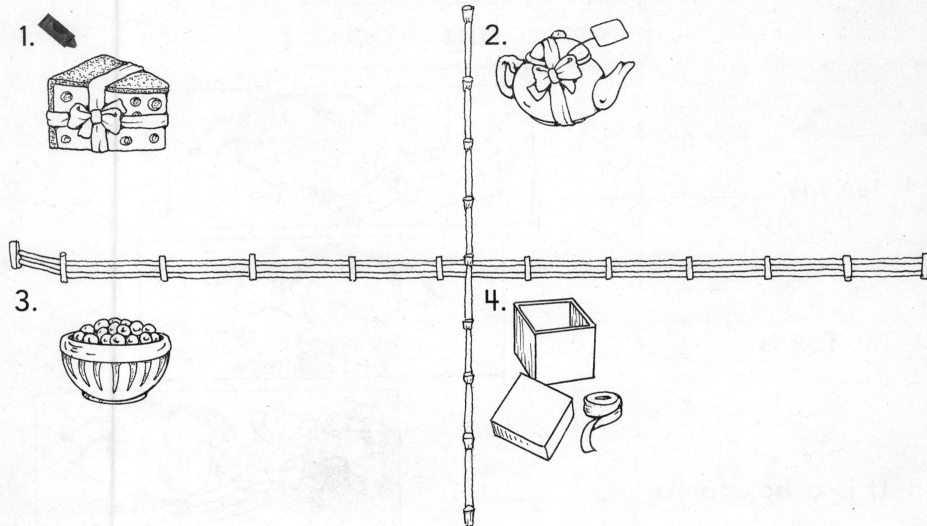

1.

2.

3.

4.

THEME 8: Down on the Farm
Week Two *Mouse's Birthday*
Noting Important Details, Responding

Children
- for 1, 2, 3, draw pictures of what Mouse might do with each of these birthday gifts
- for 4, draw a picture of what they would like to give Mouse and what Mouse would probably do with that gift

 Home Connection
Let me tell you the story my teacher read to us today. It's *Mouse's Birthday.* Then I'll tell you about the gifts Mouse got and what I would give him.

239

Name _____

fox   big   box

 _____

1. See my _____ .

_____

2. My fox is _____ .

_____

3. It is a box for a _____ .

 THEME 8: Down on the Farm
Week Two
Phonics: Short *o* and Short *i* Words

Children
• read the sentences and write words to complete them

 Home Connection
Let me read these sentences to you. We can cut out the words at the top into separate letters, scramble them, and build the words again.

240

Copyright © Houghton Mifflin Company. All rights reserved.

Name _____

b   s

	o	x
	i	t

Fox ran to a big _____ .

See Fox go to the box and

_____

_____ .

THEME 8: Down on the Farm
Week Two
Phonics: Short *o* and Short *i* Words

Children
• write letters to complete the picture names (*box* and *sit*)
• write each word to complete the sentences

Home Connection
Ask me to read these sentences to you. Then let's take turns making up other things Fox could do with a box.

241

Name _____

the   said

1. _____

"I see _____ fox," said
Pig.

2. _____

"I see the pig," _____
Fox.

3. _____

"I see a box," _____
the pig.

4.

The fox can not see

_____ pig.

THEME 8: Down on the Farm
Week Two
High-Frequency Words Review *the, said*

242

Children
• read the cartoon sentences and write *the* and *said* to complete them
• draw the pig in the place he is hiding for the last sentence

Home Connection
Ask me to read this cartoon to you. Then I'll tell you about why Fox couldn't see the pig.

Name _____

1.

2.

3.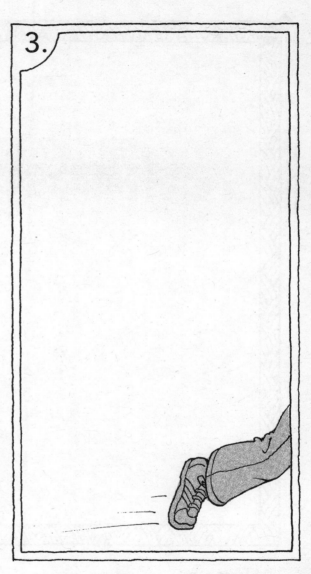

THEME 8: Down on the Farm
Week Three *A Lion on the Path*
Drawing Conclusions

Children
- for 1 and 2, color the picture of what the cat or the rabbit is trying to get away from
- for 3, draw a picture of what they themselves might run away from

 Home Connection
The story *A Lion on the Path* is about a farmer who gets away from a lion by tricking it. Let me tell you how he did that.

Name _____

1.

2.

THEME 8: Down on the Farm
Week Three *A Lion on the Path*
Responding

Children
1. think about what the rabbit in the story might do after it jumps into its hole and draw a picture of their idea
2. think about what the lion in the story might do after the rabbit gets away and draw a picture of their idea

 Home Connection
I made up more for the story *A Lion on the Path* and I drew pictures. Let me tell you about my pictures.

244

Name _____

1.

2.

3.

THEME 8: Down on the Farm
Week Three
Phonemic Awareness Review: /h/, /f/, /s/

Children
for each row,
- color the Alphafriend and two pictures whose names start like the Alphafriend's name (*Hattie Horse*, *Fifi Fish*, or *Sammy Seal*)
- draw another picture at the end of the row that starts with the same sound

 Home Connection
Let me tell you about these Alphafriends and why I colored the pictures beside them. Then I'll tell you about the pictures I drew.

245

Name _____

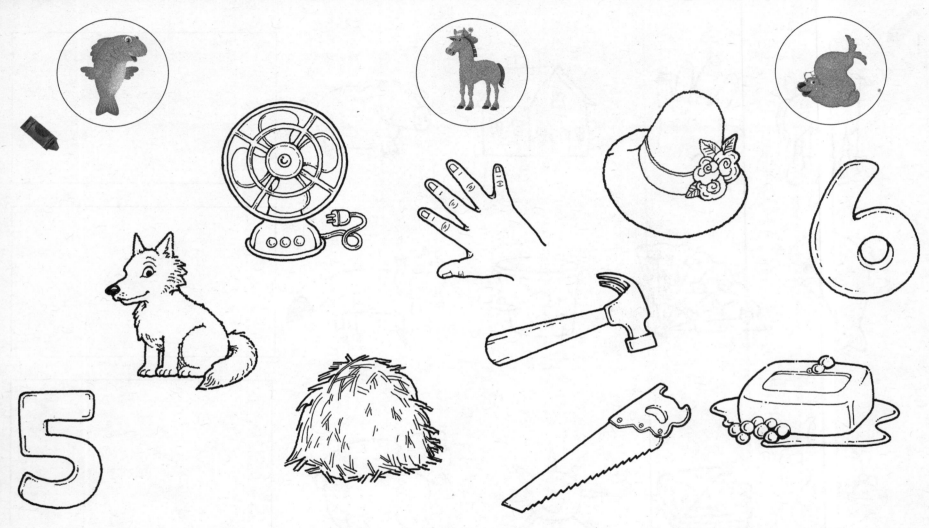

THEME 8: Down on the Farm
Week Three
Phonemic Awareness Review: /h/, /f/, /s/

Children
color the pictures and
- draw lines from *Fifi Fish* to the things that start like her name
- draw lines from *Hattie Horse* to the things that start like her name
- draw lines from *Sammy Seal* to the things that start like his name

 Home Connection
Please help me find pictures in books and magazines of some things that start like *Hattie Horse, Fifi Fish*, and *Sammy Seal*.

Name _____

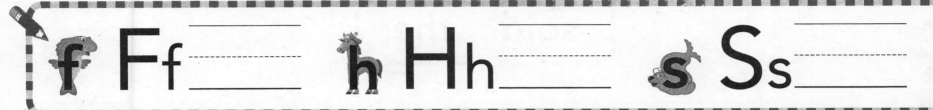

f Ff _____   h Hh _____   s Ss _____

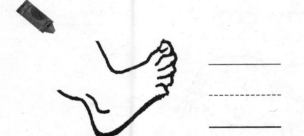 _____

 _____

 _____

 _____

 _____

 _____

THEME 8: Down on the Farm
Week Three
Phonics Review: Initial Consonants _h, f, s_

Children
• name each Alphafriend and letters at the top
• write the letters _Hh, Ff,_ and _Ss_
• color the pictures and write the letter for the sound they hear at the beginning of each picture

 Home Connection
Please help me write the letters _h, f,_ and _s._ Then we can hunt for things or pictures whose names begin with the sounds for these letters.

247

Name _____

said the

1. _____

"I have _____ box," said Nan.

2. _____

"Here is my cat," _____ Nan.
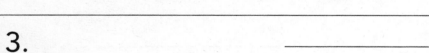

3. _____

"I like the box," _____ the cat.

4. _____

Nan said, "It is _____ box for my cat."

THEME 8: Down on the Farm
Week Three
High-Frequency Words Review *said, the*

248

Children
• read the sentences and write *said* or *the* to complete them
• color the pictures

Home Connection
Ask me to read this short story to you. Then we can look through some books together to find the words *said* and *the*.

Name _____

1.

2.

THEME 8: Down on the Farm
Week Three *Mouse's Birthday*
Drawing Conclusions, Responding

Children
1. draw some of the guests and something that happened at Mouse's party
2. draw some guests that might come to a party for the farmer and what might happen at that party

 Home Connection
We heard a story today about a mouse's birthday party. Let me tell you the funny things that happened and about the pictures I drew.

249

Name _____

pig   fox   hot

1. See the fat _____ .

2. See the big _____ .

3. See the _____ fox and pig.

THEME 8: Down on the Farm
Week Three
Phonics Review: **Short o and Short i Words**

Children
- read the sentences and write *fox*, *pig* and *hot* to complete them
- mark yes (smile) or no (frown) to show whether the pictures go with the sentences

 Home Connection
Let me read these sentences to you. Then we can cut the sentences into separate words, scramble them, and build the sentences again.

250

| h | v | b |

| | o | t |

I have a _____ pot.

| | o | x |

My _____ can fit.

| | a | n |

The big fox ran to the

_____ .

THEME 8: Down on the Farm
Week Three
Phonics Review: Short *o* and Short *a* Words

Children
• write letters to complete the picture names *hot*, *box*, and *van*
• write each word to finish the sentences

Home Connection
Ask me to read the words and the sentences to you. Then let's try to say "Do not put the fox in the box with the pot" very fast five times. Do you think we can do that without laughing?

251

Name _____

| said | the | for | have |

1.

Nat said, "Here is the fox

_____

_____ Dan."

2.

_____

Dot _____ , "I have the

pig for Dan."

3.

Nan said, "Here is

_____

_____ cat for Dan."

4.

_____

"I _____ the van

_____

_____ Dan."

**THEME 8: Down on the Farm
Week Three
High-Frequency Words Review** *said, the,
for, have*

252

Children
• read the words at the top
• read the sentences and write the words to
complete them
• color the picture of the gift for Dan they like
best

 Home Connection
I've learned to read the words
said, *the*, *for*, and *have*. Let me
read you the sentences that have
these words in them.

Name _____

1   2   3

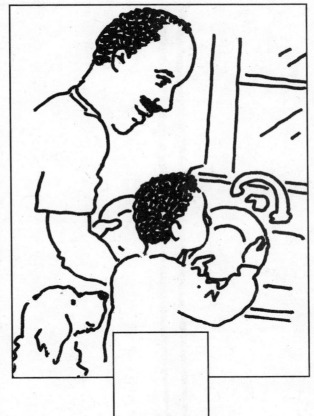

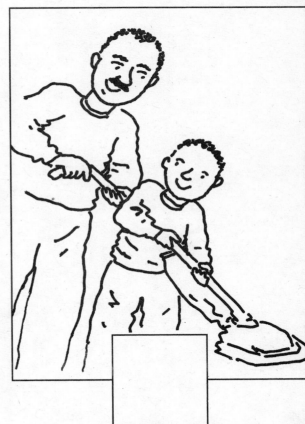

THEME 9: Spring Is Here
Week One *Kevin and His Dad*
Sequence of Events

Children
- write 1, 2, and 3 in the pictures to show what Kevin and his dad did first, next, and last in the story
- color the pictures that show the boy and his dad working

Home Connection
Ask me to tell you the story we heard today, *Kevin and His Dad*. Then we can talk about what steps we need to take to do a job at home together.

253

Name _____

THEME 9: Spring Is Here
Week One *Kevin and His Dad*
Responding

Children
- draw themselves doing a chore with a family member
- draw some objects they might use for doing different chores around home

Home Connection
Let me tell you about the pictures I drew. Let's see how many of our chores are like the ones Kevin did with his dad.

Name _____

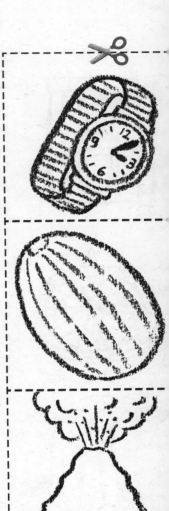

THEME 9: Spring Is Here
Week One
Phonemic Awareness: /w/

Children
- color all the pictures on pages 255 and 256 that start like *Willy Worm*
- cut and paste the pictures for that sound in the boxes on page 256
- draw something else that starts with that sound

Home Connection
Let's name some things around the house that start like *Willy Worm.*

Name _____

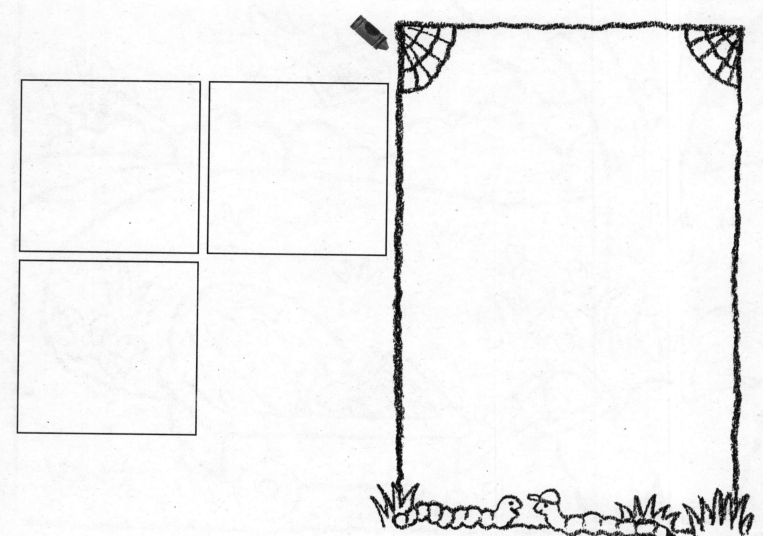

Name _____

1.  W w _____ W _____ w _____ _____ _____

2.

3.

THEME 9: Spring Is Here
Week One
Phonics: Initial Consonant w

Children
For 1 and 2, children write *w* beside the pictures whose names start like *Willy Worm*
For 3, children draw two things whose names start with *w*

 Home Connection
Today we learned the letter *w*. Let's look through magazines for pictures whose names begin with that sound. You can help me make a list of the things we find.

257

Name _____

play

1. _____

Dan can _____  .

2. _____

Nan can not _____ .

3. _____

Pat can _____ .

4. _____

Can Nat _____ ?

THEME 9: Spring Is Here
Week One
High-Frequency Word *play*

258

Children
- read the sentences and write *play* to complete them
- mark the smile (yes) or the frown (no) to show whether the pictures go with the sentences
- draw a picture for sentence 4

Home Connection
Let me read these sentences to you. Then I'll tell you about the pictures I drew.

Name _____

1 2 3

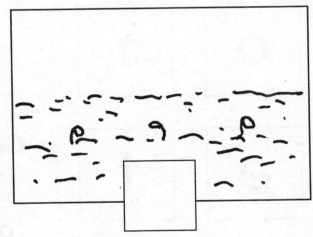

THEME 9: Spring Is Here
Week One
Sequence of Events

Children
For each row,
- write 1, 2, 3 below each picture to show what happens first, next, and last
- color the pictures that show what happens last
- think of a story for each row of pictures

 Home Connection
I wrote 1, 2, and 3 on the pictures to show what happens first, next, and last. Let me tell you a story I thought of for each row.

259

Name _____

| w | p | h |

| | e | t |

Do not let the cat
_____
get _____.

| | o | t |

I can set the
_____

_____ pan here.

| | e | t |

Can I have a pig
_____

for a _____ ?

THEME 9: Spring Is Here
Week One
Phonics: *w*, Short *e* and Short *o* Words

260

Children
• write the letters to complete the picture names (*wet*, *hot*, and *pet*)
• write each word to complete the sentences that go with the pictures

 Home Connection
Let me read these sentences to you. We can cut the letters apart to build *wet*, *hot*, and *pet* again.

Name _____

v	e	t
F	o	x
g	e	t

_____

_____

_____

_____

_____

_____

Can you _____ to the cat?

The _____ can see my pet.

I can not see _____ yet.

Children
• blend and write the words *vet*, *Fox*, and *get*
• write these words to complete the sentences that describe the pictures

Home Connection
Ask me to read these sentences to you. Then help me think of some words that rhyme with the words I wrote.

Name _____

play said the

1. _____

"I can play," _____
the cat.

2. _____

"I can _____ ,"
said the pig.

3.

"I can not play," _____

----

said _____ fox.

4.

See the cat and the pig
play.

THEME 9: Spring Is Here
Week One
High-Frequency Words Review **play, said, the**

Children
• read the sentences and write *play, said,* or *the* to complete them
• draw a picture to go with sentence 4

Home Connection
Listen to me read this cartoon. Then we can cut it apart and put it together like a book. After we make a cover for it, I can read it to someone else.

262

Name _____

1.

2.

THEME 9: Spring Is Here
Week Two *The Tortoise and the Hare*
Characters/Setting

Children
1. circle the pictures that show who the story was about
2. color the picture that shows where the story happened

 Home Connection
Ask me to tell you the story, *The Tortoise and the Hare*. Then I'll tell you about the pictures of who was in the story and where it all happened.

263

Name _____

 1.

2.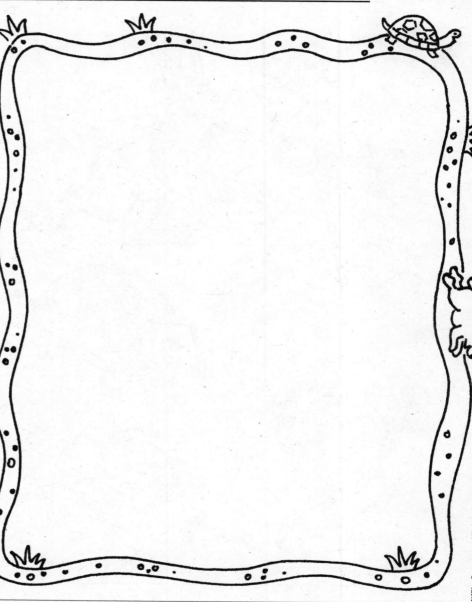

THEME 9: Spring Is Here
Week Two *The Tortoise and the Hare*
Responding

Children
1. choose and color a character Hare might want to race with the next time
2. draw their own picture of this new race

 Home Connection
While you're looking at my picture, I'll tell you about who is in my story about a race and where the race might take place.

Name _____

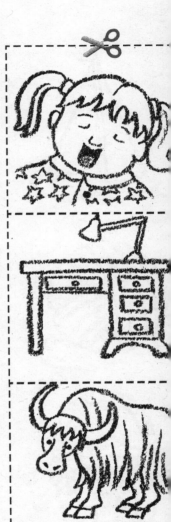

THEME 9: Spring Is Here
Week Two
Phonemic Awareness: /y/

Children
- color all the pictures on pages 265 and 266 that start like *Yetta Yo-Yo*
- cut and paste pictures for that sound in the boxes on page 266
- draw something else that starts with that sound

Home Connection
Let me tell you which pictures start like *Yetta Yo-Yo*. Then we can look around the house for yellow things — *yellow* starts like *Yetta Yo-Yo*.

265

Name _____

Name _____

1.

2.

Y y

THEME 9: Spring Is Here
Week Two
Phonics: Initial Consonant y

Children
1. draw lines from pictures whose names start with the sound for *y* to *Yy*
2. write *Yy* at the top and draw something else for that sound in the box with Yetta Yo-Yo

 Home Connection
The next time we go for a walk, let's look for things whose names begin with the sound for *y*.

267

Name _____

she

Nan

Jan

Nan said _____ can go.

Jan said _____ can not go.

THEME 9: Spring Is Here
Week Two
High-Frequency Word *she*

Children
• read the sentences and write *she* to complete them
• complete the face pictures at the top to show how each girl feels
• draw a picture to go with each sentence

 Home Connection
I can read these sentences to you and tell you about the pictures I drew. Then let's think of other sentences with the word *she* in them.

Name _____

THEME 9: Spring Is Here
Week Two *Mrs. McNosh Hangs Up Her Wash*
Characters/Setting, Responding

Children
- draw the person this story is about
- draw some things she hung on her clothesline and some of the things she saw around her clothesline as she worked

 Home Connection
Would you like me to tell you a funny story I heard today? It's called *Mrs. McNosh Hangs Up Her Wash*. Can you guess who the story is about?

269

Name _____

| hen   pen   box |

1.

_____

Can a _____ fit here?

2.

Can fit in the _____ ?

3.

_____

Can the _____ fit in the hat?

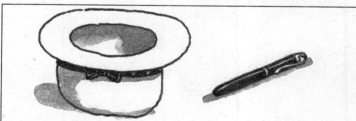

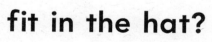

THEME 9: Spring Is Here
Week Two
Phonics: Short _e_ and Short _o_ Words

270

Children
- read the questions and write words to complete them
- mark the smile (yes) or the frown (no) to show their answers to the questions about the pictures

Home Connection
Let's write _hen_, _box_, and _pen_ on a piece of paper. Then I'll make up sentences with these words and you can write my sentences.

Name _____

| h | D | m |

| | e | n | I see the _____.

| | e | n | The _____ sat and sat.

| | o | t | _____ and Dan

have the pen.

THEME 9: Spring Is Here
Week Two
Phonics: Short _e_ and Short _o_ Words

Children
• write letters to complete the picture names (_men_, _hen_, and _Dot_)
• write each word to finish the sentences

Home Connection
Let's cut out the letter squares, mix them up, and build the words _hen_, _Dot_, and _men_ again. Can you help me make up other sentences with these words?

271

Name _____

1. _____

_____

"I can play it," _____

said.

2. _____

_____

"I can _____ it,"

she said.

3. _____

_____

She _____, "I can

play the  ."

4.

And I said, "I can play

_____

_____

Children
- for 1 and 2, read the sentences and write *she,*
  said, and *play* to complete them
- for 4, write *the* and draw a picture to finish the
  sentence

Home Connection
Ask me to read these sentences
to you. Then I can tell you
about the picture I drew in 4.

Name _____

THEME 9: Spring Is Here
Week Three *The Three Billy Goats Gruff*
Categorize and Classify

Children
• color yellow the things for Little Billy Goat, red for Middle Billy Goat, and blue for Big Billy Goat
• draw something else in three different sizes for the three goats

 Home Connection
Today we heard a story called *The Three Billy Goats Gruff*. Let me tell it to you. Listen for what each one says to the troll under the bridge and how he says it.

Name _____

THEME 9: **Spring Is Here**
Week Three *The Three Billy Goats Gruff*
Responding

Children
- draw something they would like to see on the big hill
- draw someone under the bridge
- draw someone on the bridge

Home Connection
Let me tell you about the pictures I drew. Then let's make up a story about my pictures and figure out a way to get to the hill besides over the bridge.

274

Name _____

1.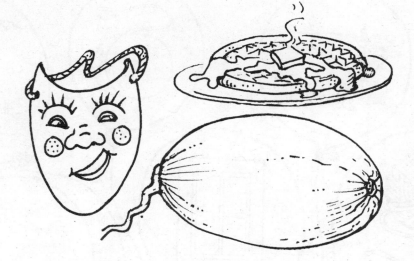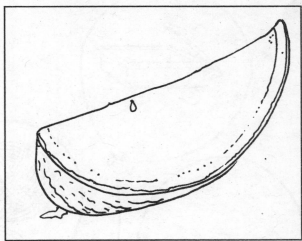

2.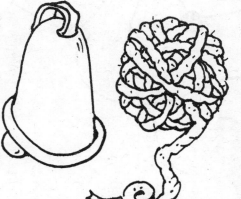

THEME 9: Spring Is Here
Week Three
Phonemic Awareness Review: /w/

Children

1. color the pictures whose names begin like *Willy Worm* and complete the watermelon picture

2. color the pictures whose names begin like *Yetta Yo-Yo* and complete the yak picture

 Home Connection
Let's name all the things on the page that start like *Willy Worm* and *Yetta Yo-Yo*. Then we can find words in a book that start the same. You can read the words to me.

275

Name _____

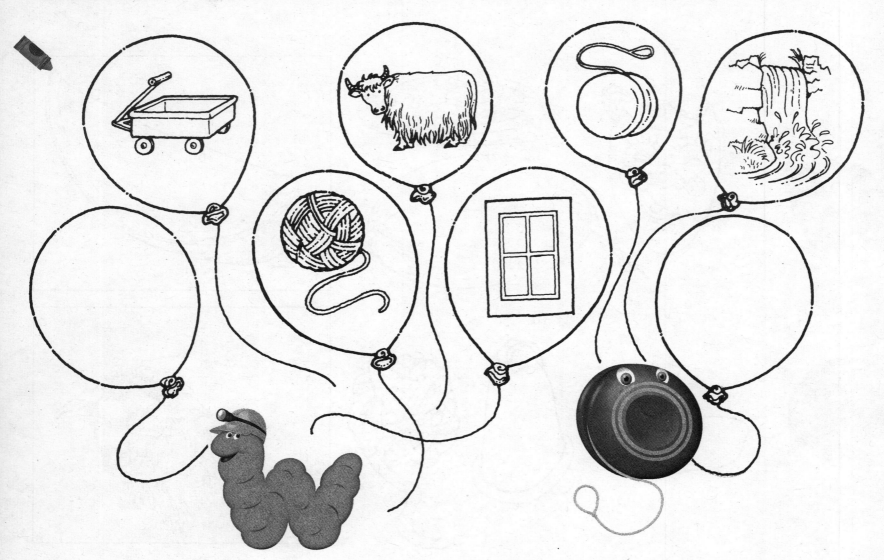

THEME 9: Spring Is Here
Week Three
Phonemic Awareness Review: /y/

276

Children

- color blue Willy Worm's balloon and all the pictures that start like *Willy Worm*
- color yellow Yetta Yo-Yo's balloon and all the pictures that start like *Yetta Yo-Yo*

 Home Connection
Let's play this game: I'll say, "blue balloon" or "yellow balloon." Then you name something that starts like *Willy Worm* for blue or something that starts like *Yetta Yo-Yo* for yellow.

Name _____

Ww **Y**y

THEME 9: Spring Is Here
Week Three
Phonics Review: Initial Consonants *w, y*

Children
- name the letters at the top
- name the pictures *Willy Worm* and *Yetta Yo-Yo* think about
- color and write *w* or *y* next to the pictures whose names start with the sounds for those letters

 Home Connection
Next time we drive somewhere, let's look for things whose names start with the sounds for *w* or *y*.

277

She   play

1.

_____

Can my cat _____ ?

2.

_____

_____ can play.

3.

Can my big pig

_____

_____ ?

4.

_____

_____ can not play!

278

Name _____

THEME 9: Spring Is Here
Week Three *Mrs. McNosh Hangs Up Her Wash*
Categorize and Classify

Children
- color things to wear yellow
- color things to eat red
- draw and color one more thing to wear and one more thing to eat that Mrs. McNosh could hang on her line

 Home Connection
Can you figure out why I colored some of the things yellow and other things red? Let's name more kinds of things to wear and more kinds of things to eat.

Name _____

 e **n**

The pen is for the
_____
- - - - - - - - - - - - - - - -
_____ .

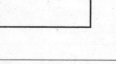 **o** **t**

The big van is
- - - - - - - - - - - - - - - -
_____ here yet.

 e **t**

The big van is here
- - - - - - - - - - - - - - - -
and it is _____ .

 THEME 9: Spring Is Here
Week Three
Phonics: Short e and Short o Words

280

Children
- write the letters to complete the words *hen*, *not*, and *wet*
- write each word to finish the sentences

 Home Connection
We can cut out the letter squares, mix them up, and use them to spell *not*, *wet*, and *hen*. Then we can find the matching picture for each word.

Name _____

| pot   ten   wet |

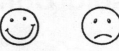

1. _____

Is the fox _____?

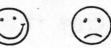

2. _____

Is the _____ hot yet?

3. _____

Can _____ men sit here?

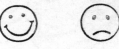

THEME 9: Spring Is Here
Week Three
Phonics: Short *e* and Short *o* Words

Children
• look at the pictures, read the questions, and write words to complete them
• mark the smile (yes) or the frown (no) to show their answer to the questions

Home Connection
I can read these sentences to you! We can write the letters *e*, *t*, *n*, *o*, *p*, *t* and *w* on separate scraps of paper and use them to build the words I wrote again.

Name _____

| play   she   said   the |

1. "Here is my play kit," _____

_____ Nan.

2. _____

_____

"I like the _____

kit," said Dan.

3. _____

"Jan said _____ can

get ten hats."

4. "Jan can get the hats for

_____

_____ play," said Dan.

THEME 9: Spring Is Here
Week Three
High-Frequency Words Review: play, she,
said, the

Children
- read the sentences and write *play*, *she*, *said*, or *the* to complete them
- color the pictures

 Home Connection
Let me read you these
sentences. Then let's make up
other sentences with these words
in them. Will you write down
our sentences so I can find the
words *play*, *she*, *said*, and *the*?

Name _____

THEME 10: A World of Animals
Week One Run Away!
Beginning, Middle, End

Children

- think about what happened at the beginning and at the end of the story

- draw a picture in box 2 that shows something that happened in the story after Little Rabbit started running away and before all the animals went back to sleep again

 Home Connection
Let me tell you the story *Run Away*! I'll point to the pictures as I tell that part of the story.

283

Name _____

THEME 10: A World of Animals
Week One Run Away!
Responding

Children
1. draw a picture to show what Little Rabbit thought was chasing him
2. think about something besides the wind in the tree branches that might have frightened rabbit and the other animals and draw a picture of your idea

Home Connection
Today we heard a story called _Run Away!_ I can tell you about it while you look at my pictures.

THEME 10: A World of Animals
Week One
Phonemic Awareness: /j/

Children
- color all the pictures on pages 285 and 286 that start like *Jumping Jill*
- cut and paste the pictures for that sound in the boxes on page 286
- draw something else that starts with that sound

Home Connection
Let's name some things around the house that start like *Jumping Jill*.

285

Name _____

THEME 10: A World of Animals
Week One
Phonemic Awareness: /j/

1.

2.

j J j   J   j

J j

J j

THEME 10: A World of Animals
Week One
Phonics: Initial Consonant _j_

Children

1. draw lines from pictures whose names start
   with the sound for _j_ to _Jj_

2. draw something else for that sound in the box
   with Jumping Jill

 Home Connection
Can you help me look through
magazines for pictures of things
whose names begin like _Jumping
Jill?_

Name _____

are

1.

Dan and I _____ at

the  .

☺ ☹

2.

Dan and I _____ hot.

☺ ☹

3.

Jan and Nat _____ at

the  .

☺ ☹

4.

Jan and Nat _____ not

hot.

THEME 10: A World of Animals
Week One
High-Frequency Word *are*

Children
- read the sentences and write *are* to complete them
- mark the smile (yes) or the frown (no) to show whether the picture goes with the sentence
- draw a picture to go with sentence 4

Home Connection
I've learned to read the word *are* and I wrote it to finish the sentences in this short story. Let me read it to you.

288

Name _____

1   2   3

THEME 10: A World of Animals
Week One Splash!
Beginning, Middle, End; Responding

Children
- think about what happened in the story and color the picture of what happened at the beginning
- write *1*, *2*, and *3* below the pictures to show what happened at the beginning, in the middle and at the end of the story

 Home Connection
Today we heard a story called *Splash!* I'll tell it to you. I'll hold up one finger when I'm telling the beginning, two fingers when I'm telling the middle, and three fingers when I'm telling the end.

289

Name _____

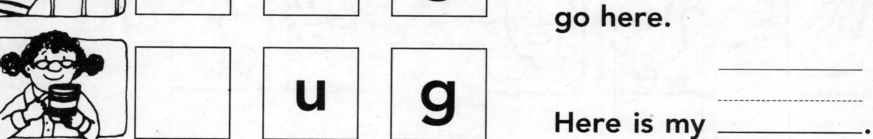

| j | m | p |

See my _____ cat.

The big _____ can go here.

Here is my _____ .

THEME 10: A World of Animals
Week One
Phonics: _j_, Short _u_ and Short _e_ Words

Children
• write letters to complete the picture names (_pet, jug, mug_)
• write each word to complete the sentences that go with the pictures

 Home Connection
Let's think of some words that end with the sounds at the end of _pet, jug,_ and _mug_. Then we can make up some silly rhymes with the words.

Name _____

| g | b | j |

 **u** **g**

Can she see the _____?

 **e**  **t**

Can she _____ the pet?

 **u** **g**

Can the _____ fit here?

THEME 10: A World of Animals
Week One
Phonics: Short *u* and Short *e* Words

Children
- add letters to build the words *bug*, *get*, and *jug*
- write each word to complete the sentences that go with the pictures

 Home Connection
Let me read these sentences to you. Then maybe we can draw more pictures to go with the words *get*, *bug*, and *jug*.

291

Name _____

Are   play   she

1. _____

_____

I can _____ the hen.

2. _____

_ _ _ _ _ _ _ _ _ _ _ _ _ _ _ _

Jan said _____ can play the cat.

3. _____

_ _ _ _ _ _ _ _ _ _ _ _ _ _ _ _

_____ Dan and Nan here?

4. Dan can play the pig.
Nan can play the fox.

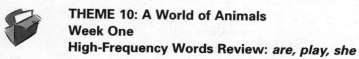
Children
- read the sentences and write *play*, *she*, and *Are* to complete them
- draw a picture to go with the sentences in 4

Home Connection
I've learned to read the words *are*, *play*, and *she*. Let me read this short story to you. Then we can make up an ending for it using the words I wrote.

Name _____

THEME 10: A World of Animals
Week Two *The Tale of the Three Little Pigs*
Compare and Contrast

Children

- compare the houses and color two things that are the same on all three
- find and circle something on the houses that is different on all three
- put a red mark on the house in the story that was the strongest

 Home Connection

Today we heard a story called *The Tale of the Three Little Pigs*. Do you know that story? Let me tell it to you. I'll try to use different voices for the pigs and for the wolf.

293

THEME 10: A World of Animals
Week Two *The Tale of the Three Little Pigs*
Responding

Children
- draw a picture of a house they would have built to protect themselves from the wolf or from a big, bad storm

Home Connection
Let me tell you about the strong house I drew. Do you think it's strong enough to keep the wolf out? What do you think the wolf might say when he can't blow my house down?

Name _____

1.

2.

3.

THEME 10: A World of Animals
Week Two
Phonemic Awareness Review: /l/, /b/, /c/

Children

1. color the pictures whose names start like *Larry Lion* and complete the leopard picture

2. color the pictures whose names start like *Benny Bear* and complete the boat picture

3. color the pictures whose names start like *Callie Cat* and complete the cake picture

 Home Connection
Let me name the pictures I colored. Then you can help me think of other things whose names start like *Larry Lion*, *Benny Bear*, and *Callie Cat*.

295

Name _____

THEME 10: A World of Animals
Week Two
Phonemic Awareness Review: /l/, /b/, /c/

Children
- color red Larry Lion's balloon and the pictures whose names start like *Larry Lion*
- color blue Benny Bear's balloon and the pictures whose names start like *Benny Bear*
- color yellow Callie Cat's balloon and the pictures whose names start like *Callie Cat*

 Home Connection
I'll name the picture on each balloon, and you can name the matching Alphafriend.

Name _____

Ll   Bb   Cc

THEME 10: A World of Animals
Week Two
Phonics Review: Initial Consonants *l, b, c*

Children
- color all the pictures
- write *l* beside pictures whose names start like *Larry Lion*, *b* beside pictures whose names start like *Benny Bear*, and *c* beside pictures whose names start like *Callie Cat*

 Home Connection
I'll tell you which pictures start with the sounds for *l*, for *b*, and for *c*. Next time we go somewhere, let's look for other things that start with these sounds.

Name _____

he

_____

Dan said _____ can fit.

_____

Nat said _____ can not fit.

THEME 10: A World of Animals
Week Two
High-Frequency Word *he*

Children
- read the sentences and write *he* to complete them
- color the pictures

Home Connection
Let me read these sentences to you. Then we can make up more sentences with *he* and you can help me write them.

298

Name _____

1.

2.

THEME 10: A World of Animals
Week Two *Feathers for Lunch*
Compare and Contrast, Responding

Children
- think about how cats and birds are different
- color red the things the cat might like and yellow the things the bird might like
- draw something both cats and birds might like

 Home Connection
Next time we take a walk, we can compare the animals we see. We can compare their sizes, their colors, their markings, the sounds they make, and what they are doing.

299

Name _____

cut   hut   Jen

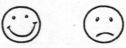

Can you _____ a pan?

_____ can go, but I can not.

She ran to a _____ .

 THEME 10: A World of Animals
Week Two
Phonics: *c,* **Short** *u* **and Short** *e* **Words**

Children
• read the questions and write *cut, Jen,* and *hut* to complete them
• mark the smile (yes) or the frown (no) to show their answers to the sentences

 Home Connection
Let's write *cut, Jen,* and *hut* on separate scraps of paper. Then we can turn the words face down and take turns picking one and making up a sentence with that word.

Name _____

b	u	t
c	u	t
p	e	n

_____

_____

_____

_____

I like the box _____ not the hat.

Is the pet in a _____?

"I can _____ it," said Nan.

THEME 10: A World of Animals
Week Two
Phonics: Short _u_ and Short _e_ Words

Children
• blend and write the words _but_, _cut_, and _pen_
• write each word to complete the sentences that go with the pictures

 Home Connection
Let me read these sentences to you. Then maybe we can draw more pictures to go with the words _but_, _cut_, and _pen_.

Name _____

| he | Are | she | play |

1. _____

Is _____ a cat?

2. _____

Is _____ a fox?

3. _____

_____ Nan and Nat

here?

4. Nan and Nat are

_____

at the _____.

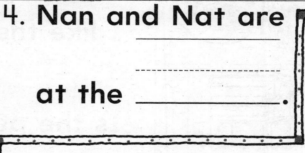

THEME 10: A World of Animals
Week Two
High-Frequency Words Review: *he, are,*
she, play

302

Children
- read the sentences and write *he, she, are,* and
  play to complete them
- draw a picture for sentence 4

Home Connection
Let me read these sentences to
you. Then let's make up a new
story about Nat and Nan who
are in the play instead of just
watching it.

Name _____

THEME 10: A World of Animals
Week Three *Henny Penny*
Plot

Children
- think about what happens in the story and draw a line through the two pictures in the story map that show something that did not happen
- draw a picture that shows what Foxy Loxy probably hoped would happen in the end

Home Connection
I can use the story map to help me tell you about the problem the animals had in the story *Henny Penny*. Then I'll tell you how they solved their problem.

303

THEME 10: A World of Animals
Week Three *Henny Penny*
Responding

Children
- think about and draw what Foxy Loxy did for his dinner after Henny Penny and her friends got away

Home Connection
Let me tell you about my pictures.

Name _____

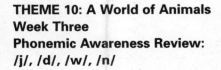

THEME 10: A World of Animals
Week Three
Phonemic Awareness Review:
/j/, /d/, /w/, /n/

Children
• color the pictures on pages 305 and 306 whose names start like *Jumping Jill*, *Dudley Duck*, *Willy Worm*, or *Nyle Noodle*
• cut and paste pictures whose names start like these sounds in the boxes beside their matching Alphafriends on page 306

🏠 **Home Connection**
Let's look in our kitchen cabinets to find things whose names begin like *Jumping Jill*, *Dudley Duck*, *Willy Worm*, or *Nyle Noodle*.

305

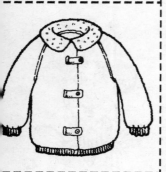

Name _____

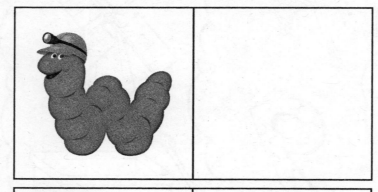

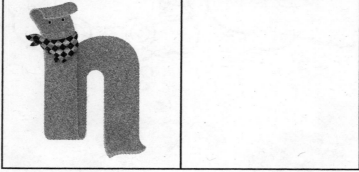

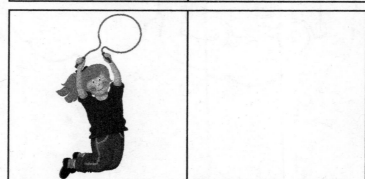

Name _____

1. **Jj   Dd   Ww   Nn**

2.

3.

THEME 10: A World of Animals
Week Three
Phonics Review: Initial Consonants *j, d, w, n*

Children
1. name the letters at the top
2. write *j, d, w,* or *n* beside the picture whose name begins with the sound for that letter
3. circle a letter at the top and draw two more things that start with the sound for that letter

 Home Connection
Let's name the pictures on the page and tell the letter each begins with. You can do the things that begin with the sound for *d* and for *w* and I'll do the ones for *n* and for *j*.

307

Name _____

He   Are   are

1. _____

Nan and Nat _____ at the van.

2. _____

_____ Dan and Pat here?

3. _____

_____ is here but she is not.

4. _____

Pat and Cat _____ at the .

THEME 10: A World of Animals
Week Three
High-Frequency Words Review: *are, he*

Children
- read the sentences and write *he* and *are* to complete them
- draw a picture for sentence 4

Home Connection
Let me read these sentences to you. Then let's make up a new story about Nat and Nan who are riding in a van.

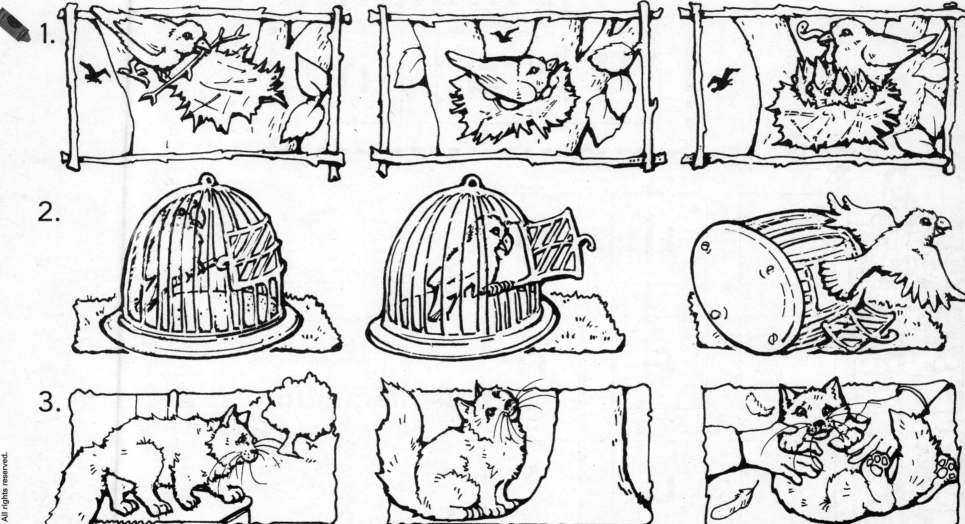

1.

2.

3.

THEME 10: A World of Animals
Week Three *Feathers for Lunch*
Plot, Responding

Children
- color the pictures in the row that shows what happened in *Feathers for Lunch*
- think of a story they could tell for each of the other rows of pictures

 Home Connection
Let me tell you a story for each row of pictures. The first row is about a story I heard called *Feathers for Lunch*. Then maybe you can tell me a different story for each row of pictures.

309

Name _____

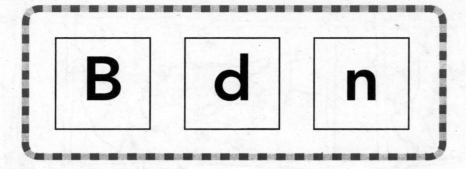

B   d   n

 u   g
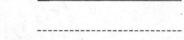

I _____ and got a box.

 e   n

Is the jug for _____ ?

 u   t

I have a _____ for the .

 THEME 10: A World of Animals
Week Three
Phonics: Short *u* and Short *e* Words

310

Children
- write the letters to complete the picture names (*dug*, *Ben*, and *nut*)
- write the words *dug*, *Ben*, and *nut* to complete the sentences

 **Home Connection**
Ask me to read these sentences to you. Then we can cut out the letter squares, mix them up, and use them to make *Ben*, *dug* and *nut* again.

Name _____

rug   nut   Ken

Is the _____ for Dan?

Is the _____ for the cat?

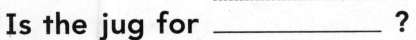

Is the jug for _____ ?

THEME 10: A World of Animals
Week Three
Phonics: Short *u* and Short *e* Words

Children
- read the questions and write words to complete them
- mark the smile (yes) or the frown (no) to show whether the pictures answer the questions

 Home Connection
Let's make up some more questions like the ones on this page. Can you think of any other words that end like *rug* or *nut* that we could use in our questions?

311

Name _____

are   He   play   she

1. Is Nan here and can

_____

_____ play?

2. _____

_____

She can _____ but

Nat can not.

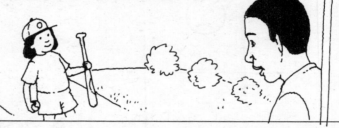

3. _____

_____

_____ is at the  .

4. _____

_____

Nan and Jan _____

here to play.

**THEME 10: A World of Animals
Week Three
High-Frequency Words Review:**
are, he, play, she

Children
- read the sentences and write *she*, *play*, *he*, and *are* to complete them
- draw a picture to go with sentence 4

Home Connection
Let me read these sentences to you. Then let's make up some more sentences for this short story. You can write the sentence down so I can look for these words in them.

312

Name ______________________________

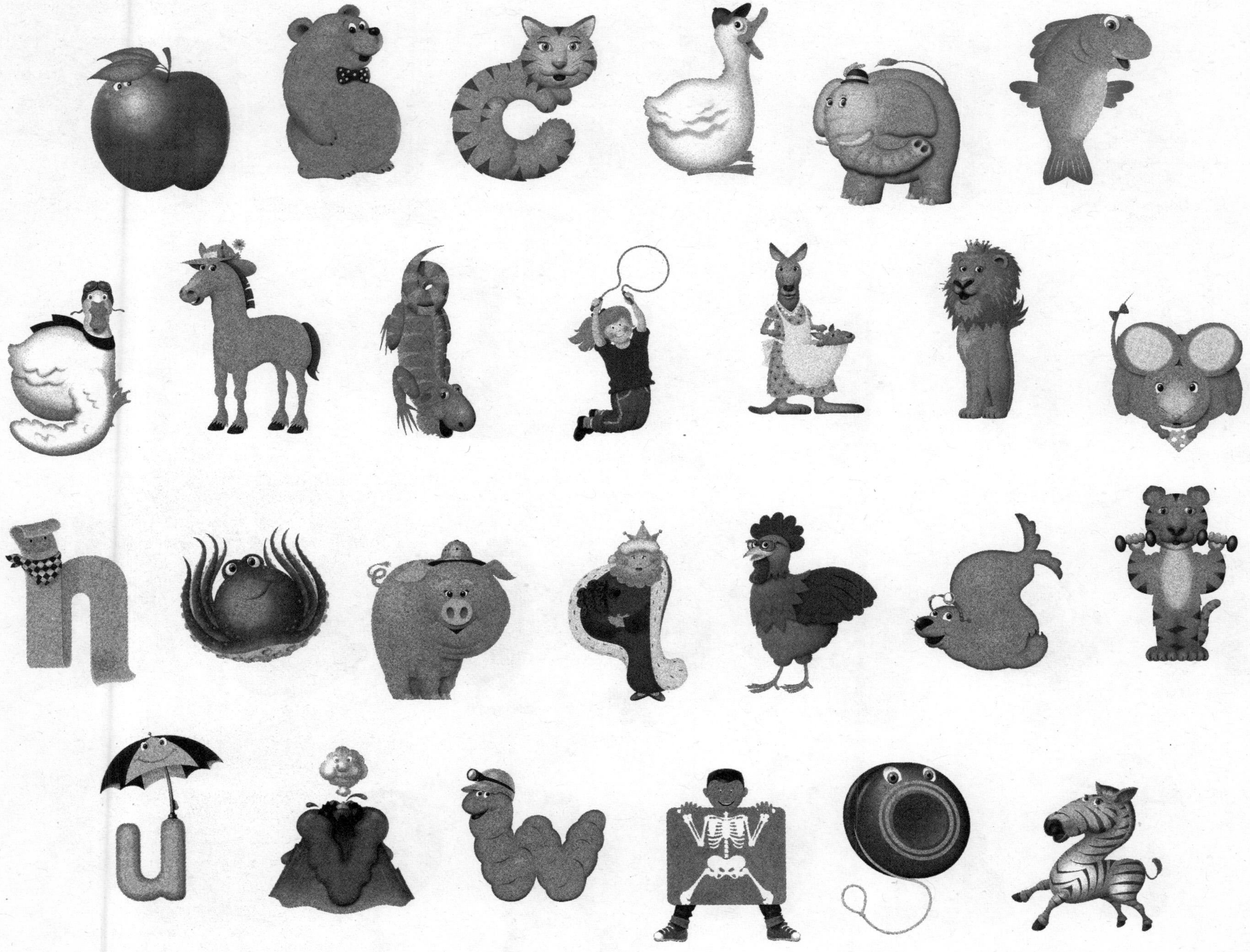